· OPENING AWARENESS ·

Opening Awareness

A guide to finding vividness in spacious clarity

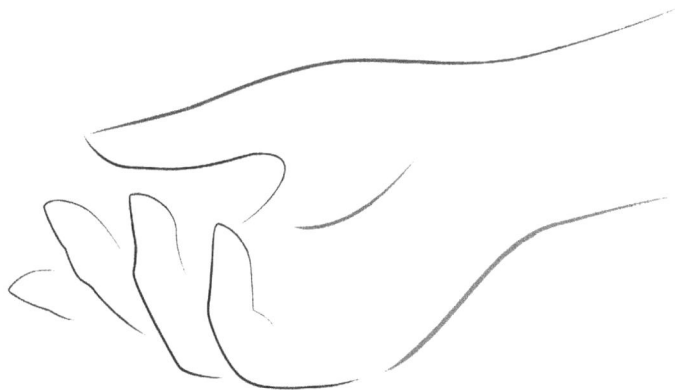

CHARLIE AWBERY

With illustrations by Jared Janes

Evolving Ground · 2023

Evolving Ground Limited
6114 W 28th Ct.
Edgewater CO 80214
www.evolvingground.org

First edition, 2023

ISBN 979-8-9866286-0-8

Opening awareness

Opening awareness is a path of meditation that leads to better ways of being in the world: passionate, accurate, and spontaneous.

As your mind settles and your senses open, you discover new freedom and purpose in everyday activities. Skillful perception, creative choice, and confident action are hallmarks of practice.

Opening awareness transforms your relationship with your emotions, and so your relationships with others—and this makes all the difference, for family, work, and society.

Life becomes a dance of creative engagement as vividness in spacious clarity pervades experience.

COMMUNITY

Evolving Ground

Evolving Ground is a global community exploring a transformational path of passionate involvement with the world.

Our life-affirming approach empowers creative, effective individuals: people who lead with courage, kindness, and grace. Our methods are contemporary adaptations from traditional Vajrayana. They train confidence within uncertainty, responsible autonomy, and flair.

Community participation promotes spacious, productive engagement with everyday life. We develop healthy, enjoyable, fruitful relationships with ourselves, with our families, friends, and coworkers, and with our projects and societies.

Opening awareness meditation enables vaster, brighter, freer ways of seeing, feeling, and acting. That makes it the foundation for all our other practices.

To learn more and to join, visit www.evolvingground.org. You can also read about Evolving Ground's programs in the *What's Next* chapter at the end of this book.

TABLE OF

Contents

Opening awareness	v
Evolving Ground	vi
Why practice opening awareness	1
What makes opening awareness different	3
Life-affirming view	4
An experience of spacious-self—not no-self	6
Discovery without stages	7
How to practice	9
How do you remain uninvolved?	10
Finding spacious clarity	15
Establishing familiarity	17
Practicalities: previewing the rest of this book	21
How to sit comfortably	25
Find a stable position	25
Acknowledge and address pain	33
Scaffolding practices	35
Finding awareness in breathing	37
Counting breaths	37
Finding awareness in sensation	38
Finding awareness in sounds and light	38
Visualization	39
Expanding sensory awareness	40
Walking awareness	41
Including inside and outside	42
Building your own scaffolding	43

Addressing common difficulties   44

Risks and safety   44

Thoughts are not enemies of awareness   46

Will I stop thinking clearly?   47

Sleepiness   48

Restless agitation   49

Boredom   50

Frustration with slow progress   51

Splitting, burnout, and rebellion   52

Dissociation   53

Weird side effects   55

Emotional turbulence   57

Therapy and opening awareness   57

When emotions arise, welcome them   59

Expanding your emotional range   62

Energy troubles: depression and overexcitement   70

Spacious involvement in life   75

Awareness in interactions   76

Communicating with integrity   77

Spontaneous action   78

Emotional and ethical maturity   79

Leading   81

Transitioning from other meditation paths   82

What's next?   87

More resources   88

Acknowledgements   91

About the author   93

Why practice opening awareness

Opening awareness is a meditation path that leads to *spacious clarity*: experiences of continuous, vivid appreciation of what is happening.

As you begin to have more space around thought in your meditation, moments of quiet presence arise elsewhere in life. At times, you may experience a brilliant clarity, unobscured by compulsive rumination. This spacious awareness makes previously inhibited choices available. You may find new ways to respond, as you see emotional and relational patterns more clearly.

Opening awareness embraces ordinary life.

Some meditation methods train detachment from emotions and dissolution of the self. Opening awareness, by contrast, welcomes the texture of emotional experience, and fosters versatility in self-perception.

Once you have established familiarity with opening awareness you may find:

- Courage to stay present and spaciously engaged in any circumstance, however unexpected or challenging

- Moments of effortless, quiet awareness while you are involved in ordinary activities

- Vividness: heightened awareness of sounds, sights, sensations—your world becomes colorful, vibrant, and clear

- Intimate familiarity with previously-unnoticed "textures" and physical sensations associated with your emotions

- Confidence in meaning and purpose

- New spontaneity and responsible autonomy in relationships: family, work, projects, and society

- General contentedness punctuated by moments of irrationally exuberant joy

These are common effects, though none are guaranteed: opening awareness varies in its reach and impact among individuals. You may experience such effects soon after starting to practice regularly.

> *"Opening awareness creates a space of no judgment and total freedom to experience anything that arises. I enjoy that each sit will be uniquely different. I love surprises."*
>
> —Kristie, Evolving Ground apprentice

This book is a detailed, practical manual for opening awareness meditation. If you apply the suggestions here consistently and regularly, you can establish an ongoing daily practice. That will bring noticeable changes to the quality and availability of awareness in your sitting practice within a few months, or perhaps even only weeks.

> *In the same way that practicing a physical activity will grow your strength and agility even before you are comfortable with the new movement, practicing opening awareness can bring benefits to your day-to-day life even before you feel you've mastered the instructions.*

What makes opening awareness different

Meditation is not "all one thing." There are many systems of meditation, which differ in techniques—and also in goals and results. Different systems produce different alterations in conscious experience, and different transformations in your self and the way you feel and act in the world.

The technical methods of a meditation system propel you on a *path* that heads in a particular direction. The many meditation techniques available are not just different means for achieving a single, shared purpose.

Different paths have different end points. Do you want to go where this one can lead you?

A good initial reason for meditating is often curiosity: a desire to explore unusual, extreme forms of consciousness. What experiences will a particular meditation method give rise to?

Some different outcomes various systems promise include:

- Non-self, or True Self, or Cosmic Oneness
- Unchanging content-free consciousness without sensory awareness—or vivid perceptual awareness in dynamically evolving situations
- Immunity to suffering—or compassion for the inevitable suffering of all sentient beings, including oneself

3

- Concentrated, focused attention control—or panoramic, open awareness

These words describe contrasting experiences. Which seem most attractive to you now? Why?

In the longer run, many meditators find themselves motivated more by the changes meditation brings to their way of life. Meditation methods transform your psychology, your perceptions in everyday life, and your approach to action. Different methods aim for quite different, often quite radical changes in living. Some, pursued seriously, point to permanent withdrawal into a monastery or solitary meditation hut. Others lead to richer, more effective involvement in family, projects, and society. Do you want the lifestyle a particular system encourages?

How does a meditation method work? How does it produce the results it promises? Is that believable? Is it desirable?

These are valuable questions to explore before choosing how to meditate. This chapter introduces some ways to understand opening awareness in contrast to other meditation paths that you might encounter. Understanding differences may help you decide which fits best with your preferences and circumstances.

LIFE-AFFIRMING VIEW

A meditation system's *view* profoundly shapes its goals, and so its path, and so then its methods. "View" is a term for an overarching collection of assumptions about how the world is and what meditation is for.

Contemporary society has inherited many different, sometimes incompatible views from multiple eras and cultures. Ancient views may remain implicit in a meditation system, informing its attitudes and goals. Making views explicit draws attention to potential internal contradictions. It may reveal unexpected ways a path is incompatible with your own views and purposes.

In Evolving Ground we draw attention to two broad categories: renunciative views and life-affirming views.

Many religious systems are *renunciative*: they see everyday life as inherently impure, and so to be abandoned. Most meditation methods originally evolved for renunciative purposes in renunciative settings.

They were designed to help you sever human relationships, in combination with a life of celibacy and abstinence in a monastery. Meditation was meant to enable a metaphysical escape from a cycle of suffering and rebirth by withdrawing from all connection with the defiled and defiling world. The aim was enlightenment: a state of eternal perfection, free from the emotional turbulence of ordinary life.

> *Opening awareness is not designed for cloistered, monastic life. It is accompanied by a life-affirming view, and is designed to help you experience aliveness and connection in relationships.*

A *life-affirming view* regards emotions and self, suffering and enjoyment, relationship and involvement in practical affairs as natural and pervasive aspects of human experience. Opening awareness practice prepares you for *spacious involvement* with all life's circumstances— work, family, and society. This spacious involvement is the basis for enjoyable, useful activity in the world.

The renunciative view accompanying a meditation method may sometimes go unnoticed. How do you know when a worldview is implicitly renunciative? If emotions, self, and suffering are seen as inherently problematic obstacles, and it aims to overcome them with meditation, that's a sign of a renunciative view.

Most widely-available meditation methods, ancient religious ones and modern secular ones, were devised to subdue emotions by detaching from them altogether. "Non-attachment" and "letting go" commonly describe such renunciative methods. The purpose may be to "calm the mind."

> *"It wasn't until I realized how lonely and frustrating it was for my wife being married to the equanimous, distant version of Jared that I started to wonder if there was a different way to approach my mediation practice."*

—Jared Janes, Evolving Ground cofounder

By contrast with renunciative methods, opening awareness *clarifies* the mind so that the full range of physical and emotional experience is available without conceptual elaboration. With a life-affirming attitude, any experience you encounter is welcome.

Spacious clarity includes everything that arises in experience, without ignoring, rejecting, or cutting it off. No sound is distracting, no thought is bad, no experience is wrong. Emotions and sensations come and go in awareness. Disturbing thought-stories and images gradually dissipate when they have space to do their own thing.

As your mind clears while maintaining awareness of everything you perceive, you feel more connected with the world, not less. In this experience of vivid connection, everything seems immediate and fresh.

Developing this friendly attitude towards everything that arises in your sitting practice will have positive repercussions in your relationships. Although opening awareness is most often a solitary practice, its aim is relational transformation, and beyond that social transformation.

This is a path of celebration, of down-to-earth realism, of uplifting courage, of gentle precision, and of open hearts.

An experience of spacious-self—not no-self

Many meditation paths emphasize a changing experience of the self. *No-self*, *egolessness*, *selflessness*, and *empty self* describe states of disintegration, deconstruction, or transformation in self perception.

The experience of the self in opening awareness is not emphasized over any other experience. Awareness does increase experiential understanding of the transitory, nebulous nature of all phenomena, including your self. Opening awareness emphasizes increasingly vivid, appreciative experiences of *relationship*—with your environment, sensations, emotions, perceptions, and other people and living beings.

Things, including selves, don't come with labels. We add those in order to navigate our world. That often makes experiences, including our selves and relationships, seem more fixed than they are. Opening awareness practice makes this labeling, "referencing" process increasingly obvious without denigrating it. There is nothing *wrong* with labeling, identification, and referencing that would mean we should want less of it in our day-to-day experience. Instead, opening awareness brings spacious clarity to self-perception, so you can become more adaptable, flexible, fluid, responsive, and free.

As your experience with opening awareness deepens you will come to recognize your personal patterns of reaction and response. These patterns normally dictate how you are in the world, and how others perceive you. Seeing your patterns clearly in meditation loosens their grip and increases choice in the moment. Spacious clarity, the result of opening awareness, is free from compulsive response.

When spacious clarity arises naturally in everyday circumstances, new ways of being present themselves. Your self does not disappear, as though it were a separate entity erased from experience. How you are, and how you relate, emerges in fresh responses to evolving contexts.

Discovery without stages

Opening awareness is more like exploring a wide, varied terrain than following a fixed path.

Many meditation systems offer a straight, narrow, well-paved path. They provide way stations you are supposed to reach, in the correct order, to be given the next set of technical instructions. This sort of rigorous, progressive, staged approach can be helpfully reassuring.

By contrast, although opening awareness has some typical intermediate results, there is no prescribed series of stages. Personal journeys through meditation to spacious clarity are diverse. Everyone starts with a unique pattern of awareness and unawareness from which to expand experience. For example, some people have odd proprioceptive side effects early on. Others never experience this. Some do experience unexpected, sudden shifts in bodily awareness, but only after years of practice.

The challenge is that the breadth and openness of the practice can seem overwhelming.

Until you have some familiarity with spacious clarity, opening awareness may seem confusing, imprecise, or vague. In progressive systems, the method is reassuring but the result can be disorienting. This is opposite to opening awareness! Opening awareness can seem elusive at first, but the result is reliable. Spacious clarity is consistent and predictable, more so than anything else in life. Many practitioners have said that their meditation became immensely reassuring after their first experience.

Another challenge in opening awareness is that, even though you can learn from others, *nobody can tell you exactly what to do*. This is the nature of discovery. The more you meditate, the more you will hone your personal understanding of how to find and maintain awareness. In the long term your meditation is the sum of your personal confidence and trust in this process. Talk to peers, mentors, and experienced practitioners while you establish familiarity.

> *"I see everyone as being in a vast spiritual territory, each with unique perspectives and experiences of the regions they've explored. In Evolving Ground, through opening awareness, practitioners find their way to a basecamp in this territory, which equips them for their life-affirming path. Since everyone finds themselves at a different starting point, each journey to basecamp is different. When practitioners connect on their journeys, they find that appreciating each others' views and skills makes personal discovery possible."*

—Jared, Evolving Ground cofounder

How to practice

The method is simple: sit down and *remain uninvolved* with whatever arises.

This may seem paradoxical at first. The overall aim of the path is passionate engagement with the fullness of life. That is the opposite of uninvolvement! However, opening awareness leads to spacious clarity, within which we perceive all of life with new, more vivid accuracy. We can find that spacious clarity in every other activity. Opening awareness trains us, through remaining temporarily uninvolved during practice sessions, to find clarity even while fully involved.

This book is a detailed manual on how to put that training into practice in meditation. However, remaining uninvolved is the whole of the method. Everything else is context and preparation for simply and completely remaining uninvolved.

Remain uninvolved... with what?

With anything, with everything.

Ordinarily we find ourselves involved with experience automatically. For example, an itching sensation arises on the skin and we scratch it without conscious choice. Similarly, we can't resist elaborating whatever is occurring in our minds—by multiplying ideas, thought-stories, and imaginings. We focus attention on whichever thoughts seem most important. "Remaining uninvolved" is to experience whatever is happening without engaging, elaborating, focusing, or acting in response.

As elaboration subsides—but awareness remains—experience becomes unexpectedly simple, clear, and immediate.

HOW DO YOU REMAIN UNINVOLVED?

Remaining uninvolved is a guiding principle that may change in appearance according to circumstance. It is not a specific technique; not a fixed tool that looks the same whenever it is applied.

For example, remaining uninvolved with angry thoughts may require some patience, whereas remaining uninvolved with drowsiness needs fresh alertness. Practice in remaining uninvolved in different circumstances leads to a particular experience that becomes familiar, despite the differences in details.

Although common questions about confusions and difficulties arise, the most helpful answers may not be the same for everyone. There are no step-by-step instructions, because the process of remaining uninvolved is individually and circumstantially unpredictable. Instead, I recommend you intelligently adapt the guidance in this book to suit your aims, personality, and circumstances.

To engage in this way means that, even if and when you seek support and guidance, you are owning your role as the arbiter of your practice. In each practice session, you can take responsibility for your present state, and choose how to proceed.

This approach requires integrity—and it develops integrity, too. You become more attuned to notice the nuance of your changing state, and to respond appropriately. Exercising personal choice according to circumstances is like flexing a muscle: in this case, a muscle that helps you see and respond more clearly.

When you begin practicing, *remaining uninvolved* relies on effort and intention. Gradually, as you become more experienced, it requires less. Eventually, you may find remaining uninvolved happens naturally, without any work at all.

Include everything in awareness

Remaining uninvolved requires an intention: to stay present and alert without manipulating whatever arises in your experience. Remaining uninvolved is "maintaining awareness while…" rather than "detaching from…" or "observing."

During meditation, mental and sensory events occur. These events take many forms—narrative thoughts, visual thoughts, bodily sensations, emotions, sounds internal and external, conceptual maps of sensations, analysis, sleepiness, irritation, boredom, excitement, and so on.

In opening awareness, all these events come and go. The practice is to notice them without preference or judgment, to experience them in whatever way they may appear. Remaining uninvolved is simply to continue to notice all of this happening.

In opening awareness, you do not need to stop, cut off, ignore, or actively reduce thoughts or sensations.

Instead, include them in awareness. Experience them as they come and go. The process of remaining uninvolved is one of discovering, allowing, noticing, including, and welcoming everything that arises in experience. There is space for everything in awareness to be as it is.

See if you can rest in the experience of everything as it arises, without losing awareness. Whatever occurs, let it occur. Refrain from focusing on anything in particular. Allow everything to come and go of its own accord.

This practice is preliminary training for finding awareness *during* engagement in life—including difficult circumstances like repetitive arguments, unexpected setbacks, and unfulfilled longings.

Hold an intention

Spacious clarity dawns as a gap between thoughts.

Your overall intention for sitting practice directs your meditation as it occurs. Intend to stay with a gap whenever one appears. Holding that intention for your meditation practice can subtly change the experience of the gap and your capacity to rest there when it happens. Because you hold an intention for your meditation practice, when a gap appears, you're more likely to be able to stay with it.

You can't force your thoughts to clear, but as you become more familiar with remaining uninvolved, moments of thought-free awareness arise more frequently and fulfill your intention to remain present without mental elaboration of experience.

While remaining uninvolved is difficult at first, *intending* to remain uninvolved is a simple thing, which you can always do when you sit down to meditate. Your intention can be the subtle, persistent force that helps you discover spacious clarity, even when your meditation is challenging.

This is not the same as trying to *create* space between thoughts. Notice how conceptual elaboration hastens to fill your moment of spacious clarity. You could notice the quality of those thoughts which crowd into the space of awareness. Thoughts often have a "flavor," or an "atmosphere." Without analyzing, can you notice how they are, in passing?

Immersion is involvement

Noticing that you have been lost in thought or sleepy dullness is awareness emerging from oblivious immersion. Stay alert and attentive to what happens as you notice awareness returning. What happens just before awareness reemerges?

Interest is involvement

Although opening awareness may clarify your understanding of your own mind, it is not a deliberate inquiry. If you notice curiosity about your emotional, cognitive, or perceptual processes, you could let them be instead.

If, for instance, you notice yourself thinking "who is doing the thinking?", leave that thought without further involvement. There is no need to actively look for anything.

See if you can maintain awareness, experiencing everything as it comes and goes, without encouraging, without analyzing, without judging.

There is no need to turn the spotlight on any experience in order to promote, interrogate, or intensify it. Let it flow.

Ignoring is involvement

Remaining uninvolved does not mean ignoring.

Imagine lying in a tent, hearing the sounds of the night outside. They take place in your field of experience: you are neither straining to hear sounds, nor actively shutting them out. So long as you remain aware of experience as it arises, *potential* for involvement is available, even while it is suspended. Lying in your tent, if you heard an animal in distress, you could decide to become involved and help it. By contrast, ignoring experience eventually shuts it out of awareness completely, until there is no potential for involvement.

If you notice you are cutting off thoughts, relax. See if you can maintain awareness of the space within which thoughts occur.

If you notice you are cutting off sounds, relax. Let the sounds remain.

If you notice you are losing touch with physical sensations, relax. Notice what is happening in your body.

A conducive eye posture

Let your eyelids hang nearly closed, so that only a small amount of light shows.

> *There is a position at which the eyelids naturally settle when your spine is upright and your posture is still, comfortable, relaxed, and alert.*

This eye posture is conducive to finding periods of continuous awareness. We think more, and faster, with our eyes wide open. We notice sights in the environment and become interested. On the other hand, allowing in a little light is conducive to remaining alert. Our minds tend to quiet and settle when we close our eyes. The small amount of light prevents falling into a dull stupor.

It can take months to find the sweet spot. It is common for your eyelids to tremble until they become used to the position. Gradually build up your familiarity with the eyelid posture. Notice if you are straining your eyes and relax your focal mechanism. It's okay to relax into a soft-focused, open-eyed posture or to close your eyes while you are getting used to opening awareness. Notice how changing your eye posture affects your experience.

There is no right or wrong regarding this unusual eye posture.

Many meditators struggle to find and stabilize it. It is worth persevering, because once familiar it can quickly help you become still, mentally relaxed, and alert. However, it's nice-to-have, and not crucial.

Release, not concentration

Opening awareness is superficially similar to some other meditation methods, including secular mindfulness and techniques from renunciative Buddhist traditions. Initially, it might seem nearly the same as their concentration practices. However, those typically focus inward, starting with the breath.

Opening awareness' method and aim are quite different. Remaining uninvolved releases focus from any preference, towards all-encompassing awareness. As you gain familiarity with the practice, you will find it increasingly dissimilar to concentrative techniques.

The way you think and talk about meditation will affect the results you get. Try using the phrase "find awareness in..." rather than "focus on...", because the latter is more likely to lead to disconnectedness. "Finding awareness in the breath" (a technique described later in this book) may sound not much different from "focusing on the breath." It may be difficult at first to find the distinction between the two. However, over months and years these produce quite different results.

Intense concentration on the breath or on parts of the body, ignoring anything outside the focus of observation, leads to deep, internal absorption. It promotes *dissociation*: mental awareness separated from embodied responsiveness.

Opening awareness does not involve this trance-like intensity.
The process is evermore inclusive, rather than exclusive.

Remaining uninvolved over long periods leads to spacious clarity: an experience of vast, vivid, embodied awareness. Remaining aware, without preferential focus, *releases* you into a relaxed, clear state of mind.

This *opening into vastness* is visceral. It can feel like untightening a grip that you didn't know was tense.

FINDING SPACIOUS CLARITY

The result of opening awareness is present and boundless, a state of mind in which no thoughts arise. This is *spacious clarity*.

Your first taste of spacious clarity may only be a glimpse. You notice a gap in mental activity; but then immediately thoughts crowd back in. It's not unusual for commentary *about the gap* to derail the experience.

The first extended experience of spacious clarity is often described as beginning suddenly and unexpectedly. It is like "a bubble popping," or "a veil lifting I hadn't known was there," or "a door opening."

At first this mostly happens while you are meditating. Then, spacious clarity arises spontaneously in moments during everyday activity. Eventually, spacious clarity, which was non-ordinary, becomes a feature of your ordinary, everyday life. Becoming intimately familiar with spacious clarity usually takes some years.

> *Effects of meditation will begin to show naturally during your ordinary activities.*

Rather than trying to control your experience all of the time, make the most of naturally arising awareness. Appreciate spacious clarity when it arises. It feels more like a discovery than an action or a decision. Notice the quality and texture of your experience. Rest in the natural clear space of awareness for as long as it remains available.

> *You cannot force spacious clarity, nor fake it.*

Opening awareness practice will be boring, upsetting, and frustrating at times. It requires many hours of consistency, discipline, gentleness, determination, and patience. Eventually, as spacious clarity begins to arise spontaneously, you will come to trust your own clear, vast, and vivid way of being.

Extended spacious clarity is a non-ordinary experience. The point of opening awareness is to become familiar with this state. You may already have experienced glimpses in moments of natural tranquility, or when you were high or tripping. Opening awareness makes spacious clarity reliably and naturally available.

Spacious clarity transforms everyday life

The method of opening awareness is remaining uninvolved; but this is *not* a general recommendation for everyday life. Life mainly requires involvement, and that is mostly a good thing. Remaining uninvolved with ordinary events is only sometimes appropriate.

Opening awareness leads to spacious, passionate engagement in situations and projects. Its aim is not disengagement, nor a consistently calm demeanor. Spacious clarity changes your experience of how things are, but it does not disrupt your capacity to deal effectively with life circumstances.

Remaining uninvolved is *practice* for life. The spacious clarity it produces during meditation finds you in the hurly-burly of everyday affairs as well. By analogy, you would not perform the downward-dog yoga exercise while shopping; nor would you practice remaining uninvolved there. However, you will find the bodily ease you gain from practicing yoga at home in a supermarket as well. Likewise, you may enjoy relaxed, vivid awareness in the canned soup aisle as well as on your meditation cushion.

Opening awareness does not require you to be the same in all circumstances. You become more comfortable with the full range of your emotional experience and expression. As spacious clarity develops, you find new ways to be with emotions, and new ways of being with other people.

> "*The question of what to do outside of the formal sitting of opening awareness is very common. One answer is—just leave experience alone—and see what is there.*"
>
> —Rory, Evolving Ground pupil

Spacious clarity makes more vivid, more accurate involvement in life possible. You gain greater freedom of choice of whether, when, and how to engage with circumstances. With that, you find a way of being that is generous, dignified, and powerful.

Spacious clarity enables personal transformation.

It brings into view the habitual patterns of perception and response that form our way of being in the world. Those limit us, making us timid, petulant, or arrogant. We lash out when threatened, and later regret it.

Transformation is not possible without first seeing. Compulsive responses, previously overlooked, become obvious with spacious clarity.

Spacious clarity does not guarantee a change in behavior, but it's a powerful foundation. It opens a door to a possibility. *Non-compulsive response* begins to characterize your interactions. You respond with awareness, grace, and ease.

With practice and guidance you can learn to expand your range of responses in everyday interactions. Kinds of training, covered elsewhere in Evolving Ground, go beyond opening awareness and spacious clarity to develop responsibility, confidence, playfulness, creativity, and effectiveness.

ESTABLISHING FAMILIARITY

Where, when and how much

There are no rules about where, when, how long, or how often to practice opening awareness.

Find somewhere to sit without too much noise. Complete silence is unnecessary and impossible, but hearing other people talking, or TV or music, may make meditation more difficult. Some types of meditation can work while listening to music, but not this one.

Opening awareness is easiest sitting upright, with minimal movement. You can start in a desk chair, which will be comfortable enough for five or ten minutes. If that becomes difficult for longer meditation sessions, the later chapter *How to Sit Comfortably* suggests alternatives.

A good time to meditate is whenever you are most alert. You may need to find when that is by trial and error. It may be first thing in the morning, or later in the day. Some people like to meditate at the quietest time of day, early morning or before going to bed for example. Notice how being alert and being quiet can occur together. They are not opposites.

Consistency is more important than duration when first establishing your practice. If you are new to meditation and find guidelines helpful, you can make your own rules for the frequency and length of your sessions, and stick to them. As the practice becomes easier with familiarity, and as you become more enthusiastic because you find it increasingly enjoyable and effective, you can sit more often and for longer.

Practice and patience

Again and again you will lose awareness as events occur. Again and again you will diminish awareness, submerging it into whatever is happening.

That's okay. Over time, over weeks and months and years, you will learn how not to feed involvement. Without involvement, thoughts dissipate and sensations move and change. As awareness strengthens, you will learn to experience the simplicity, clarity, and power of your unelaborated experience.

Before learning to remain aware, you will first *intend to remain uninvolved* and then almost immediately *find yourself involved*. This may be frustrating. It could even seem like the practice is impossibly elusive. If you find yourself in this position, simply sit with the intention to remain aware until the end of your session. With regular practice, the frequency and duration of unintentional involvement decreases.

It can take time, sometimes a year or more, to discover even the *meaning* of "remaining uninvolved." But don't despair! Acquiring mastery of any skill is slow and often imperceptible. Cultivating a friendly, patient attitude towards your own process is valuable in itself—*and* the opportunity to be present is here each time.

Just as practicing a physical activity will grow your strength and agility even before you are skilled at the new movement, practicing opening awareness can bring benefits to your day-to-day life even before you feel you've mastered the instructions. You may not notice a difference from day to day... until one day, suddenly, you see that you're no longer where you were.

Good experimentation takes time and patience. Trying out a new meditation method may not have immediate effect. It's worth spending at least a few months getting used to a method before trying something different.

> I found the duration that experiments should run really surprised me. For example, finding the eyes-slightly-open position took some months. I remember a friend commenting that one should try a method for at least a few weeks before making any decisions about it. I otherwise would have quit the experiment much sooner. Being able to reflect thoughtfully on a multi-week experiment required me setting up a way to keep track of how the experiment was going.

—Aditi, Evolving Ground solo practitioner

Getting to know the feeling

Opening awareness is a method you become increasingly familiar with over time, rather than a technique you refine progressively. It is likely that your relationship with the method will mature organically, maybe unpredictably at times.

Opening awareness does not include a set of prescribed, identifiable, achievements for you to measure your progress against. It is more like conducting an experiment by trial and error. You are likely to find a positive feedback loop between changes in your experience and confidence in your practice.

As you gain experience, you may find it helpful to recognize what remaining uninvolved *feels* like. The more you experience the effects of opening awareness, the more confidence you will gain in your capacity to know how it's going.

> Imagine the difference between going on a date with someone for the first time versus having known them, intimately, for years. The difference is due to familiarity, appreciation, shared experiences—not because you refined the dating technique.

I recommend keeping a journal, describing your deepening familiarity with the texture or "taste" of involvement and uninvolvement. Meditators use words like "thick," "lost," "muddy," "limited," "preoccupied," or "dreamy" to describe involvement in mental events; in contrast with uninvolvement which is "present," "light," "clear," "expansive," "calm," and "spacious."

Discovering your purposes in meditating

Opening awareness does not gradually and covertly implant alien purposes from a "spiritual" plane of existence in your brain. (Some other meditation systems do attempt that.) Opening awareness supports your passionate, purposeful involvement in practical situations.

Why do you think you might want to meditate? Or, if you already do meditate, why?

What are your purposes in life? What gives life its meanings?

If you practice opening awareness regularly, you will find that your answers to these questions change, clarify, and connect.

I suggest that you write and save your current answers now. Reread them periodically, and add updates as they change. In three months, a year, three years, a decade, reviewing your purposes will give insight into the transformations opening awareness facilitates.

Meditation can be hard work, and you may periodically lose track of the reasons it's worthwhile. At times when meditation feels like an unpleasant, pointless chore, rereading your motivations for starting and for continuing can reconnect you with inspiration.

Our ideas about life-purpose are commonly muddled. We are influenced by many conflicting ideologies that advocate one sort of purpose or another. We may have spent years thinking about purposes, weighing diverse arguments and considerations, trying to make sense of them in the context of our individual capacities, personality, and circumstances. The result is usually an unsatisfactory and inconclusive compromise. "What should I do with my life?" remains an irritating unsolved quandary.

You can expect questions of purpose and meaning to arise during meditation. Your thoughts will re-explore this maze of analysis—and in opening awareness, you will remain uninvolved.

When the thoughts wear themselves out, an underlying *felt sense* of meaningfulness emerges. As you become familiar, it clarifies and strengthens, and you gain a visceral confidence. This is not certainty in specific purposes themselves (though this can occur). It is confidence in *recognizing* purpose.

Initially, this provides only clarity of meaningfulness as such, without specifics. However, in your day to day experience off the cushion, visceral recognition and conceptual clarity connect. You gain certainty in specific purposes that align with your felt sense. Intellectual theories *about* purpose that lack connection with your experience of life seem of less concern.

You may find then that your purposes in meditation and your purposes in life align. The title of this section is deliberately ambiguous. You discover your purposes *for* meditating as you clarify life-purposes *by* meditating.

A supportive community

Establishing your opening awareness meditation does not require a group or a teacher. This book can give you a good start, and you can get results with consistent solo practice.

However, maintaining motivation, interest, and enthusiasm for your meditation practice over months and years may require more than a manual. Also, efficiency matters. You have chosen to meditate over other valuable uses of your time. Receiving feedback, getting help with specific problems, and reflecting on your meditation experience with others can accelerate your learning.

For these reasons, I recommend you develop a network of support, friendships, and guidance—the context in which you can thrive as a meditator. Evolving Ground is one such.

PRACTICALITIES: PREVIEWING THE REST OF THIS BOOK

You have now heard what spacious clarity is like, and what it may do for you, your relationships, and your everyday life. That may sound attractive... And if you have read this far, you have *already learned* the whole method of opening awareness and how it leads to spacious clarity. It is that simple!

It may seem *too* simple to put into practice, though. And you may run into difficulties when you try.

Most of the rest of this book is a guide to managing practical challenges. Remaining uninvolved is not easy—until you have practiced it enough to establish familiarity. Everyone runs into trouble, usually almost immediately. Common examples are:

- I keep forgetting that I'm supposed to be meditating

- After a few minutes, I have an overwhelming impulse to get up and do something else

- I fall asleep, or almost do

- I keep replaying an old conversation with my former boss—I get so angry and can't let it go

- I thought I already knew how to meditate; I know this method is supposed to be different somehow, but I can't figure out what I'm supposed to do here

- "Opening awareness" and "spacious clarity" still sound theoretical, vague, and improbable

- My back hurts

This book explains effective ways to address all such difficulties.

It is designed to be read on-and-off, multiple times. Some of its suggestions become relevant only as you encounter particular issues. They will make sense as your experience grows. Once you are familiar with the basics of opening awareness, return to the manual for troubleshooting and further guidance.

You may find it difficult to remain motionless in a chair for long. Physical discomfort may limit the length of your meditation sessions. Increasing duration opens up successive realms rarely available in less than half an hour, less than an hour, and so on. The next chapter, *How to Sit Comfortably*, suggests ways of sitting still that can be sustained for an hour or more. It explains how sitting can cause pain, and how to address it with postural changes.

Once sitting comfortably, it is good to try, as much as possible, to simply remain uninvolved with whatever arises in experience. However, you are likely to find yourself constantly losing awareness of the practice as you become involved in mental events. When this becomes frustrating, you can apply alternative methods. These are not the opening awareness practice itself, but preliminary exercises that "build the muscles" you need. The *Scaffolding Practices* chapter describes several.

The chapter *Addressing Common Difficulties* is a catalog of other challenges many meditators face, with ways to address each. These include getting lost in thoughts and reactions to thinking; restlessness and sleepiness; emotional reactions to meditating like boredom, frustration, and burnout; weird side-effects; and mental health issues.

You won't encounter all these at once, or at first. It's fine to skim that chapter, or skip it altogether, on a first pass through the book. Whenever you do run into trouble when meditating, remember that you can consult a relevant section to find a specific solution.

Strong, difficult emotions—anger, fear, sadness—arise naturally during opening awareness practice. For many meditators these present challenges, and they get their own chapter, *Emotional Turbulence*. However, opening awareness is unusual in welcoming such emotions, whereas many other meditation systems seek to control, subdue, or even eliminate them.

When they appear in spacious clarity, strong emotions transform into vivid energy, which can propel accurate, effective action. This transformation is one of the greatest, most far-reaching benefits of practice on the Evolving Ground path.

Although its method is remaining uninvolved, the purpose of opening awareness is to bring its results into passionate engagement with the fullness of life. That is the topic of the chapter *Spacious Involvement*. It describes benefits for relationship, for developing emotional and ethical maturity, and for spontaneous responsible action.

Some readers may be coming to opening awareness having already meditated in another system—vipassana, for example. The method and path of opening awareness are different, as the earlier chapter *What Makes Opening Awareness Different* explained. Naturally, experience in other systems may be more or less conducive to practicing opening awareness. Your habits of mental action may point in a different direction, in which case it could take a while to unlearn them. The chapter *Transitioning From Other Meditation Paths* gives practical advice for experienced meditators from other systems.

What's Next, the final chapter, goes beyond the content of this book. In time, you may encounter difficulties this book does not cover; or become curious about what particular meditation experiences mean; or find that meditation is changing your life in ways you'd like to understand better.

You may also want to discover how opening awareness fits into a broader system of transformative, life-affirming practices. The chapter provides pointers to relevant resources offered in Evolving Ground and elsewhere.

How to sit comfortably

Meditating requires physical as well as mental stamina.

Build the length of time you feel comfortable meditating gradually. Forcing yourself to sit for unreasonably long periods is like running a marathon without any training. Instead, nurturing courage with caution may help you find the sweet spot.

Do your best to remain still, because physical stillness will help you find mental stillness. Stillness without muscle tension means that your posture is at ease.

Some meditation systems emphasize absolute stillness because maintaining rigid discipline over the urge to move helps you enter into deep, absorbed concentration. By contrast, opening awareness prepares you for spacious clarity in everyday circumstances, in which you'll be constantly active.

> *Opening awareness emphasizes comfort in stillness above disciplined immobility. Maintain awareness while you adjust your position, rather than forcing yourself to remain still with discomfort.*

FIND A STABLE POSITION

Opening awareness does not require any special meditation posture. However, finding a stable position matters. That may take some trial and error. You will make ongoing adjustments as your body learns.

A stable position means one in which you are still, comfortable, relaxed, and alert, so you do not need to tense any muscles.

There is no perfect posture that is ideal for everyone. Age, flexibility, and past injuries will affect what works best for you.

Sit on a chair, or on the floor

Wear comfortable clothing. Loosen your belt if it is tight.

Sit either on a chair, or on a firm cushion on the floor.

You can experiment with different sorts of chairs. Adjustable desk chairs are a good starting point. Set the height so your feet are solidly on the floor. Feel the ground. Make sure the front edge of the seat does not dig into your thighs.

You may find it helpful to add a firm cushion for support, raising your hips a little above your knees. Support behind your back for the natural lordosis of your spine is also helpful until your muscles strengthen enough that you don't need it. (See the illustration.)

To sit on the floor, try a firm cushion under your butt: a *zafu*, or a buckwheat or millet cushion. Try a thick meditation mat (*zabuton*) under your knees. Feel their solidity connecting you with the earth beneath.

Do not sit cross-legged with your knees in the air. Having your knees higher than your hips when sitting pulls your lower spine from its natural alignment.

See the illustrations for three floor sitting postures that encourage the natural alignment of the spine. The first two look almost the same, but in the second, a foot rests on the opposite calf. That requires a bit more flexibility, but can be more stable. These positions both need a zafu or other support to get your butt higher than your knees.

The pretzel-shaped "lotus position" is the most stable, easiest on your back, and can support you without a cushion, but most people find it difficult. You might like to work toward it, but take it gradually and don't injure yourself.

As an alternative to a cushion, you could try a kneeling bench.

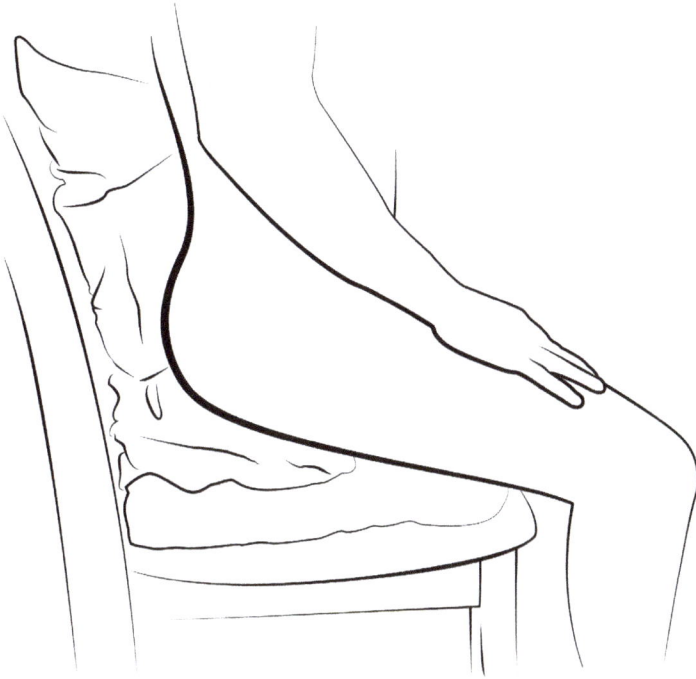

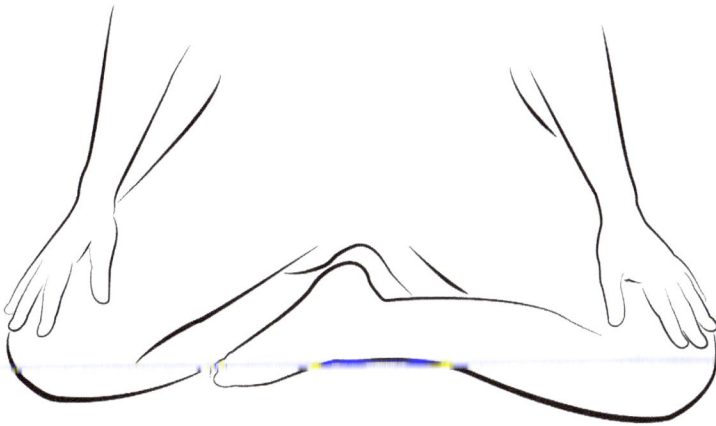

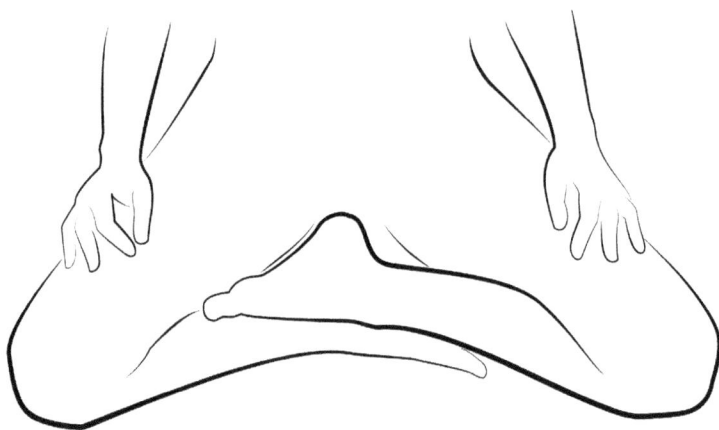

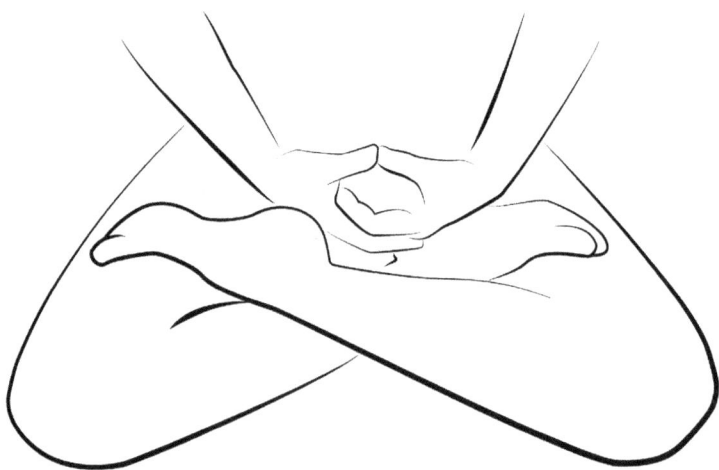

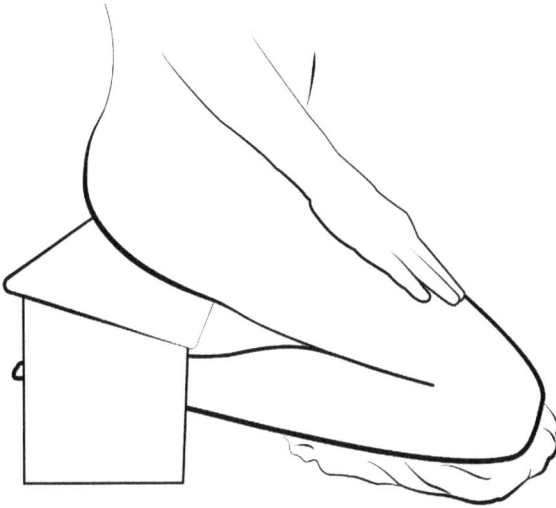

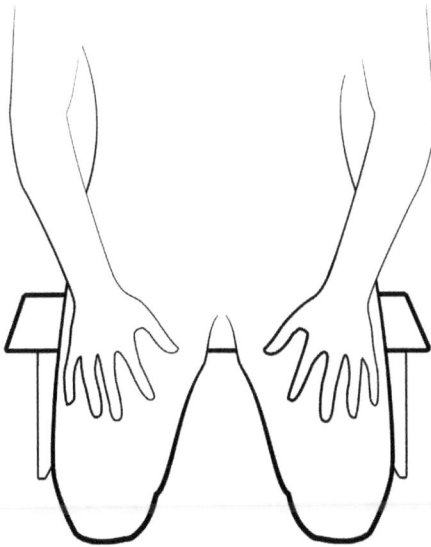

Balance your spine so it can relax upward

As a general rule, you can be comfortable for long periods only if the bottom of your butt is a bit higher than the bottom of your knees. Raising it a few inches lets your spine relax into its natural, upright position. Your thigh bones will angle slightly downward. A firm cushion beneath your butt helps, whether you are sitting on the floor or in a chair.

> *You cannot sit still, comfortably, and at ease for long with your knees above your hips. If this posture "feels normal" to you, then you have forced your spine to get used to a strained position.*

The bottom of your spine should balance effortlessly in your pelvis.

It's common, instead, to use muscular effort to hold the bottom of the spine tilted either back or forward. We do that in attempts to compensate for being off-balance due to tension in torso muscles.

The first picture in the figure below shows how a slumped-forward spine strains the upper back and neck.

Slumping can also put pressure on your sciatic nerve, causing pain in distant parts of your body as well the bit you've contracted.

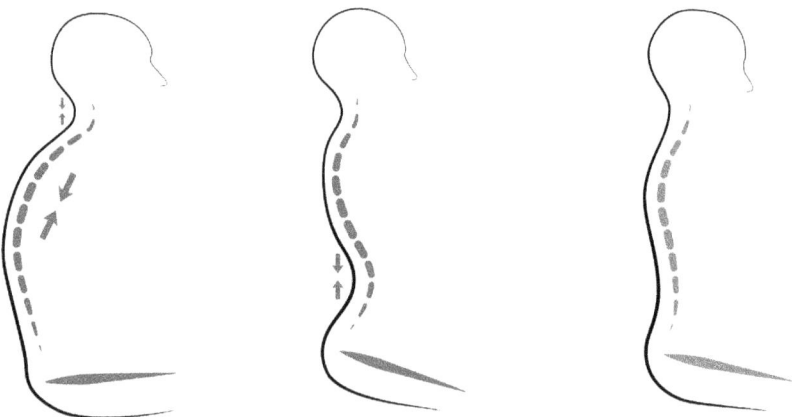

Pulling your lower back forward to adjust for the discomfort of slumping causes tension in your thighs, hips, and lower spine (as shown in the second picture).

Notice the effort in keeping your position and how your upper body pushes forward to balance the pressure on your spine.

> *If you need to adjust your spine frequently to remain comfortable, or move your legs often to stop them falling asleep, you are not yet still. If you feel tension in muscles holding your body in position, you are not yet still.*

Let the front of your hips and your spine relax apart from each other. The natural curve of the spine looks something like the third picture in the row.

Spinal misalignment in all kinds of sitting is a major cause of back troubles. If you are used to slumping in a chair or on a settee it may feel odd to sit naturally. It can take time to rebuild the muscles that support your spine.

You may eventually find that you want to extend your meditation sessions to an hour or more. It can take a year to develop the physical skill of sitting before that becomes feasible.

Release your neck

In a chair or on the floor, when you release habitual tension and allow your spine to relax and lengthen, you may feel as though your head is floating upward. This is ideal.

If your chin points up and your head tilts back, adjust your posture until there is no kink in your neck. The first picture below shows a neck kink caused by trying to get your head on the level while crunching your chest and slumping your shoulders.

Let your head gently dip into a slightly downward angle. Experiment with your neck position so that the top of your spine extends upward naturally, without strain. (See the second illustration.)

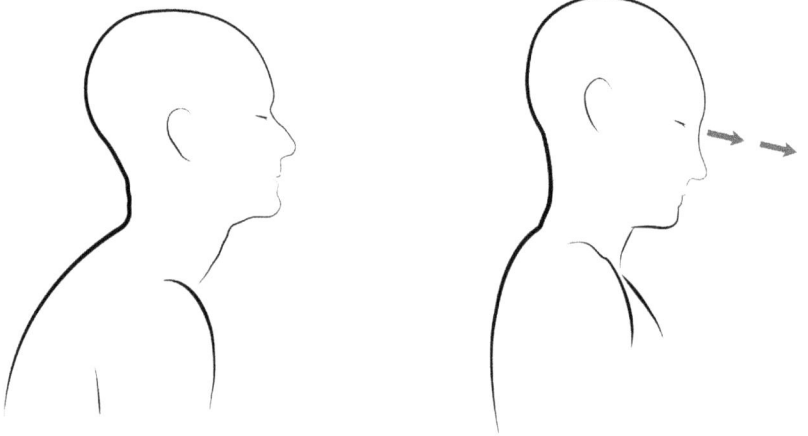

ACKNOWLEDGE AND ADDRESS PAIN

Feeling pain from postural strain is not the same as restlessness, or a strong urge to fidget. You will often feel an urge to move, with no pain present, especially when you are getting used to meditation. Getting to know the difference is part of the practice.

> *To sit without tension may take time and practice. Ideally, every time you sit, you will be physically still, comfortable, relaxed, and alert.*

Some meditation systems advocate ignoring physical pain. Ours does not.

Pain may foretell injury. Do not risk long-term physical damage by ignoring escalating pain. Appreciate your body. Do not punish yourself: if something hurts, help it to unhurt. Rearrange your posture so that you can be still, comfortable, relaxed, and alert.

Sitting through pain is recommended in systems deriving from renunciate traditions that aim to transcend physical and emotional experience. Contemporary meditation systems that advocate sitting through pain give two justifications—discipline or bliss. After many hours of disciplined sitting through intense physical pain, it can transform into a blissful sensation. After this kind of bliss you can access a state in which you are immune to the physical sensations of pain and pleasure.

That is not the aim in opening awareness. It is not necessary to ignore pain and risk injury in order to establish discipline, or to experience extraordinary states of mind and body. You will continue to experience both joy and pleasure, and painful physical and emotional sensations, at times.

The aim is to experience sensations and emotions with spaciousness. This leads to congruent, fluid response, acting with natural grace, dignity, and powerful presence. Sometimes spaciousness can catalyze a transformation of *any* physical sensation into bliss. Or it may open the door to a quiet, clear state of mind. These do not require risking physical injury.

As you learn to sit with ease, consider how "remaining unin-volved" might apply to your physical posture. You may en-joy the discovery of effortless sitting once you let your body support you naturally rather than trying to force a correct position. Does this echo the way you relate to thoughts in opening awareness?

Mild muscle aches are normal when your body is getting used to an unfamiliar posture. Stop, or shift position if you experience numbness, leg cramps, or sharp, unexpected pain.

If your head aches when you sit, notice what you are doing with your eyes. Sometimes tension caused by a hard focus causes a headache. Some people find the instruction *"relax the roots of your eyeballs"* help-ful. Notice any attempt at hard concentration and relax that. Notice if you are holding tension in your face and neck. Relax. Let your neck be free, so the crown of your head floats naturally towards the sky. Let your back lengthen and widen.

If you have back pain when you sit, try to find the angle of the pelvis at which relaxing your weight onto your sitting bones makes your spine elongate. Adjusting the height of your support cushion helps with this.

If your knees hurt when you sit on the floor, try resting them on a thick meditation mat or a buckwheat pillow. Or, move to a chair.

Notice your breathing. Adjust your position such that you are able to breathe comfortably without contracting your chest or constricting your torso.

If you experience unavoidable or chronic pain, unrelated to medi-tation, I am sorry. That sucks. Finding the most comfortable position you can is still worthwhile.

Opening awareness tends to increase awareness of physical sensa-tion, because you do not ignore or cut off from it. Include unavoidable pain in awareness with a kind and gentle attitude.

FIVE

Scaffolding practices

Simply remaining uninvolved—the actual method of opening awareness—may be difficult, or even seem impossible, at first. You will probably find yourself constantly getting caught up in thoughts, sensations, memories, perceptions, and emotions. Half an hour may go by, and you suddenly realize you had entirely forgotten your intention to remain present. Or, you may be baffled—"specifically, what am I supposed to do?"

Many alternative methods help build the capacity for opening awareness itself. These are called "scaffolding practices," because you dismantle them once your capacity to remain uninvolved is stable.

> *You may be so used to associating clarity with focus that it is difficult to remain aware without something to latch on to. Scaffolding practices help you loosen the mental grip, so you can remain present and uninvolved at the same time.*

Scaffolds come in different shapes and sizes, metaphorically. Some are strong and durable; others are lightweight, easily erected and taken down. Some are short, spontaneous reminders to remain uninvolved.

Using scaffolding practices involves some trial and error. Knowing which one to apply at a particular moment is a skill that you learn gradually. A scaffold is working to the extent that it increases your quality and duration of awareness. You may find it takes several tries to get used to it before it functions as intended—and you may want to move from one to another to find the one that's right for the way you find your mind.

Scaffolds are means to opening awareness, not ends in themselves. In principle, when applying them, remember that their purpose is to make themselves redundant. Even the most structured and tangible scaffolding is not permanent.

The scaffolding practices described here conform to the style and language of opening awareness. They lean away from the one-pointed concentration, hard focus, noting, labeling, and preferential attention common in some other meditation methods. See the earlier chapter *What Makes Opening Awareness Different* for more about why.

Regard each meditation session as a fresh opportunity. Always begin by attempting to simply remain uninvolved, present, and alert. Then find where you are, without expectations.

Applying a scaffolding practice without knowing where you are *today* cuts off the opportunity for something unexpected to happen. Yesterday you may have been lost and distracted, but today you may find your mind still and quiet. It's easy to fall into a rote habit, assuming that your practice is going to be the same for a while. Finding afresh where you are, each time you sit, is a visceral reminder of the point of opening awareness: spacious clarity. It's a reminder too of the function of scaffolding practices: merely temporary supports that address particular, temporary difficulties.

So then, once you find where you are, you can apply a scaffolding practice if one seems appropriate.

The following is a selection of the most common scaffolding practices. You can apply one or more of them in any order. As you become more experienced you will probably get used to how each feels for you, so you can move fluidly to whichever is most appropriate in the moment. But there is no "perfect" or "correct" fit. Often one or another will work. If you apply your scaffolding practices with a "light touch" they may fall away naturally when they are no longer needed. This is the ideal, but it's also fine to stop deliberately, either when the practice has worked, or when it isn't working and you want to try something else.

Try each scaffolding separately and allow time for its effects to establish themselves, before adding in others. If you add too many, too soon, you may find it difficult to distinguish the effects from one practice to another.

The first three scaffolds are described cumulatively, but you can practice them in any order, or stand-alone.

Finding awareness in breathing

The primary scaffolding practice is to find awareness in the sensation and movement of the breath.

When you "wake up" from having been lost in thought or a sleepy haze, bring awareness to breathing. As you breathe, find the presence of awareness in the sensations associated with breathing. Notice the sensation of breath moving your body. Notice the sensation of breathing in through your nostrils and the rise and fall of your abdomen. Remain aware within the experience of breathing.

There is no need to alter the length of your breath, or to breathe in any way other than what feels natural.

If thoughts arise and pull you away from awareness in breathing, come back gently. Be glad that you are here again, in the experience of your breathing.

Finding awareness in breathing may characterize your practice for most or all of your session. This may become your primary practice for days, weeks, months, or a year or more. Don't forget to start with simple opening awareness each time, and to consciously decide when to employ this additional scaffolding.

Counting breaths

Sometimes to maintain awareness you may need more substantial scaffolding. Without changing the length or intensity of your breathing, silently count each exhalation. Start by counting from one to four and back. Rest for a few breaths without counting and then repeat the process.

When you can count reliably "one-two-three-four-three-two-one" and rest, repeatedly, without losing awareness, decrease your count to three, and rest. Repeat the process until awareness is stable, then decrease your count to two. Once awareness is stable when you count "one-two-one" and rest, increase the duration between each set until you no longer need to count breaths to remain in awareness.

You may sometimes lose awareness in thoughts and then notice that you have stopped counting. Or you may forget where you are in the sequence. You may wonder whether you are counting forwards or backwards. You may find yourself on more breaths beyond the turn of the count, lulled into a reassuring, automatic regularity. Whenever you notice that you lost awareness, start from the beginning again.

Notice if you chastise yourself or become impatient for losing awareness.

See if you can locate the sensation associated with your response. Is it in your throat, your chest, your gut? Let it be there, in awareness. Give the sensation its space. Let it be however it is, for however long it stays. When you are ready, return to counting the breath.

Whenever you find counting stable and reliable, you can try finding awareness in breathing *without* counting. However, if you cannot consistently find awareness simply in breathing today, return to counting. Be patient and kind with your process. Enjoy finding awareness wherever and however it is.

FINDING AWARENESS IN SENSATION

Whenever your awareness in breathing feels stable and reliable, gently expand the field of awareness to include more. Let breathing remain in awareness, lightly. Include the rest of your body in awareness. Notice sensations coming and going. Find awareness in the physicality of your experience. Notice your connection with the ground—include in your field of awareness the sensations associated with sitting down.

FINDING AWARENESS IN SOUNDS AND LIGHT

Without losing awareness in your breathing and your bodily sensations, notice the semicircle of light under your eyelids. (Remember the eye posture section in *How To Practice*?) Include in awareness the space in front of your cheek bones and the space in front of your face.

Notice the quality of sounds.

Practice finding the most distant sounds in your environment while including the sounds in close proximity.

> *Can you include breathing, all sensations, light, and sound in awareness without preferential focus?*

VISUALIZATION

The capacity to conjure bright, vivid images in the mind's eye varies individually. Differences may depend on personal biology, so visualization works well for some and not for others.

Visualization is a practice of mental and sometimes embodied absorption. In this scaffolding practice you do not deliberately shut out information from the other senses, such as sounds or tactile sensation. Whether or not you naturally remain aware of other events occurring is irrelevant. It doesn't matter one way or another for your purpose here. What matters most is the stability of the image. Stabilizing awareness in one domain of experience is conducive to stillness in others.

Can you visualize a blue, luminous sphere a few feet in front of your forehead? If you can do this in some way or other, you can experiment with visualization scaffolding practices.

> *Getting used to visualization as a scaffolding practice for opening awareness could also function as preparation for other practices. Many methods in Vajrayana, the historical inspiration for opening awareness, use visualizations.*

With effort and intensity, bring a bright image into awareness. Stabilize and hold the image for a short while, not more than a minute or two. It can take some months of regular daily practice to get to the point you can visualize reliably, on demand, with intensity.

Here are some visualizations to try:

- A bright, white, luminous sphere a few feet in front of your forehead, about the size of a soccer ball

- Similarly a bright blue, red, or rainbow colored sphere

- A soft, red light in your heart center, filling your chest

- A small bright blue or luminous white sphere, the size of a lacrosse ball, about a foot above your head

- A field of soft, white light behind your head

- A large, clear full moon behind your head

- A bright, yellow sun shining rays into the crown of your head

When you can quickly stabilize a clear, bright sphere, practice spinning the sphere, slowly and then faster.

Experiment with the opacity of your visualization. Does the quality of your experience change when you visualize a solid, opaque form compared to a holographic, transparent form?

Practice visualization spontaneously, the moment you notice that you have lost awareness. After your visualization, return directly to opening awareness or to another scaffolding practice such as finding awareness in breathing.

Visualization is stimulating, so it is a good scaffolding to use when you are feeling sleepy or your mind is dull. It's an antidote to "screen saver mode," a common experience. That is when you have not lost awareness completely, but neither are you alert and present. You are a bit spaced out, maybe mesmerized by the patterns behind your eyelids, as though in a trance state. Nothing much is going on, but awareness is not vast, expansive, and spacious either. A clear, bright visualization can pop you into a more alert, conscious state of presence.

Expanding sensory awareness

Sensation is always present. There is so much information available through your senses: sight, sound, taste, smell, touch, physiological experience, emotional resonance, and more.

There is always more to discover in sensory awareness.

As sensory awareness expands, thoughts, concepts, and other patterns of perception become less dominant. Allow them to arise and dissipate. Notice how conceptual processes tend to habitually categorize, order, and compress sensory awareness. Notice the impulse to label, define, narrate, and explain experience. Remain uninvolved with that process. In awareness you can allow sensations of all sorts to arise without manipulation. There is so much going on, you could never pin it all down. Releasing the impulse to control and make sense of experience for a short moment in sitting may be terrifying… or it may come as a relief.

If a physical sensation—for example hunger, restlessness, or heat—limits your attention, include that experience itself within a broader space. Consider your attention like a closed hand that has grabbed onto and contracted around an object. It is a hyperactive adaptive mechanism. But right now: you are meditating. The purpose is to remain aware through uninvolvement. The grip of attention can safely release itself to a wider, vaster experience. Eventually you may experience any sensation, however strong, without conceptually defining it.

> "My mantra with any form that shows up in opening awareness is include, include, include. So if I'm having a hard time with aversion, usually because I'm feeling unsuccessful, that flavor of experience gets included with everything else going on in my experience. It's like a color tone that's present in the tapestry of experience; there's no need to separate it out from everything else. Really try to feel the texture, to taste the flavor of that tone of experience. The prompt I like is: What does that tone feel like? Then, when you feel familiar with it, recognize that it's inseparable from everything else going on in experience. It's woven in. So include, include, include."

—Max, Evolving Ground apprentice

WALKING AWARENESS

Begin walking at a relaxed, gentle pace. Without deliberately slowing down, notice the sensations in your body as you walk. Feel the ground under your feet. Notice the sensation of wind or air on your face. Notice the temperature on your skin. Become fully present, letting thoughts subside.

Notice the colors, textures, sounds, sights, and movement in your environment. Notice patterns, repetitions, lines, density, fuzziness, change.

Gradually increase the speed of your walking while continuing to appreciate sensations and the details of your experience. Let the change in speed happen naturally; don't force it.

Bring a little more vigor into your step. Swing your arms a little; move faster. Notice your heartbeat and any change in sensation while you continue to appreciate your surroundings.

When your walk has been in full swing for a while, and your heartbeat is up, you may be short of breath. Stop suddenly. Notice what changes. Stay still for a while, maintaining awareness.

Eventually, once your heartbeat is settled and you are ready to move on, begin walking again at a relaxed, gentle pace.

You can repeat this practice any number of times in a single session. If you are a runner, you can increase gradually to a run, and finish with a sprint. Continue the awareness practice while you are running.

This scaffolding practice is useful for punctuating your opening awareness session if you are on retreat, sitting for longer periods of time, or if you find sitting physically painful due to injury or illness. It's also helpful if you are "stuck" in your practice, and feel like you've been on a plateau without much change for a long time.

INCLUDING INSIDE AND OUTSIDE

Your sphere of awareness can expand outwards until it encompasses everything within reach of your senses. Practice expanding awareness outwards in all directions.

Your sphere of awareness can expand inwardly, until it encompasses all bodily and emotional sensations. Practice expanding awareness inwards from all directions.

"Internal" and "external" sensations need not remain separate. Everything you feel inside your body and everything you experience outside your body is happening in the same space of awareness. Consider that your senses in their entirety describe an unbroken field of experience. Practice bringing awareness everywhere in your experience.

After this exercise, drop any sense of intentional movement, direction, or focus. Remain uninvolved without preferential focus.

BUILDING YOUR OWN SCAFFOLDING

"Am I doing it right?" is a tempting question to ask, especially when you are learning to meditate. It is reasonable to want to know whether you are at least "on the right track." Opening awareness can seem frustrating because, although the overall system and its purpose can give you some indication about how things are going, you are always responsible for choosing whether or not to use a scaffolding practice and which to work with from one day to the next.

When you are first establishing opening awareness, you might want to get used to the scaffolding practices described here to the point that you know which ones work well for you and in what circumstances. However, the number of scaffolding practices is potentially infinite. In *How To Practice*, I described remaining uninvolved as a principle that you can engage with intelligently, rather than a set of prescribed techniques. You can take this approach to scaffolding too.

As your capacity to maintain awareness grows, you may find that supports arise naturally out of immediate circumstances. For example, suppose you notice that whenever you are ruminating on an ongoing problem your eyes' focal mechanism is strained: you discover that consciously relaxing your focus, behind closed eyelids, helps keep awareness from immersion in the problem. You have invented a new, personal scaffolding practice!

Building your own scaffolding, either intentionally or by reflex, grows from confidence in your capacity as a meditator. It can help to remember that the practice always comes back to relating to your experience, whatever it is, with integrity.

Addressing common difficulties

This chapter suggests ways to deal with diverse difficulties. It contains specific guidelines that may not be relevant unless you're experiencing particular challenges in your meditation. The details may be overwhelming on a first reading, so you may forget them almost immediately. It could be best to treat this chapter as a reference manual.

These are resources to return to in difficult times.

Some challenges, like sleepiness and restlessness, are common to all kinds of meditation, but they might have different solutions according to the method. Instructions appropriate in other meditation systems may not be the same as those suggested here.

None of the techniques discussed here are rules. They are methods designed to help you stay still, comfortable, relaxed, and alert.

RISKS AND SAFETY

Meditating has risks: physical, emotional, and psychological. These range from dissociation and derealization, depression, depersonalization, through to mania and pathological spaciness.

Many meditation methods cut you off from perceiving the world, which risks depressive or dissociative states. Opening awareness is different: it's an expansive style of meditation, which increases connectedness and vividness of experience. Therefore, its risk profile tends more toward excitement and mania.

Most meditators experience no serious threat from meditation to their physical, emotional, or psychological safety. Nevertheless, most meditators do occasionally experience physical, emotional, or psychological discomfort and change.

A very small proportion of meditators experience serious problems. If you experience any of the following, stop meditating:

- Anxiety attack

- Acute physical or neurological pain

- Unusually slow or fast heart beat

- Fainting. (Some meditation systems include an advanced stage, "cessation," that includes loss of consciousness. Opening awareness does not.)

Don't push through. Seek professional help.

Meditation is challenging and it can lead to decreased control, or loss of control, emotionally and psychologically. Opening awareness—more than some other types of meditation—works with loosening the desire to control experience. This can feel frightening. Many meditators experience episodes of tolerable overexcitement or anxiety before finding a quiet, vast, spacious clarity.

Learning to loosen compulsive control is useful for everyone and is part of the process. It is impossible to draw an exact line and say "at this point, stop." However, persistent, heightened anxiety is not usual or helpful.

You can develop your capacity to hold discomfort and to know when to stop. Learning how to do this is an aspect of the practice. It involves taking personal responsibility for your meditation and its effects, fine-tuning your perception of when to continue, and when to stop and take a break. Expect change, and expect unusual, non-ordinary experiences. There are many sources of support, advice, and help. Becoming familiar with the risks prepares you if something unexpected and unwanted happens.

Talking with peers, and with more experienced meditators, is valuable. That's especially true if you are a solitary practitioner, and pride yourself on your solo path. It's worth risking vulnerability by sharing your experience, and asking others about theirs. You may be surprised and delighted by how much difference it makes to develop friendships with others whose practice experience you trust.

There is an overview of meditation risks at vividness.live/meditation-risks.

Cheetah House provides sensitive support to people experiencing meditation-related difficulties.   Contact them if you or someone you know is not functioning due to extreme meditation effects: www.cheetahhouse.org

The rest of this chapter looks at some common issues that fall short of emergencies. These problems are unlikely to cause a serious threat to your mental health.

Thoughts are not enemies of awareness

This meditation method regards thoughts as events within awareness, not external threats to it.

> *As you notice thoughts, you can be friendly towards them, appreciating their distinctive qualities.*

Becoming lost in thought is the most common interruption to remaining aware in the present. Thought stories are like magnets, pulling awareness towards them until it is lost. The more you meditate, the more you notice the "sticky" quality of thoughts and other mental phenomena.

Remind yourself before meditating that the purpose is to remain aware. You don't want to become lost in thought, so even when the stories or ideas are magnetizing: for the duration of your sit, you will intentionally maintain awareness *by noticing* the alluring quality of thought.

When you notice the pull from your thoughts to become involved, see if you can find the "space" around them: the space that they arise into. When this is impossible, incorporate a scaffolding practice.

As you become more aware of your thinking process, you may notice reactions to thoughts. Then you may react to the reactions. Then…

At some point, the process of going meta to the current thought pattern dissolves itself. In the meantime, notice the fascination that thought has with itself.

> *Can you experience the difference between a thought and the space within which it occurs?*

When thoughts lose their magnetic quality, they seem more like sensations in the body which arise and dissipate of their own accord. With presence, you find increasingly that your thoughts arise, occupy the space of awareness, and disappear, without you having to *do* anything.

At this point, see if you can notice particularly the beginnings and endings of thoughts. What happens between one ending and the next beginning?

WILL I STOP THINKING CLEARLY?

Opening awareness does not affect your capacity to think clearly, creatively, reasonably, rationally, and with intention. On the contrary, many meditators find that their thinking capacity improves. In opening awareness, the thought process settles and seems less "sticky." Meditation frees up thinking so that, rather than running along inert habitual lines, spontaneous, unexpected creative insights occur.

> *The daily break from thought-immersion can provide relief, and render intentional thinking fresher and more alert too.*

It is tempting to capture every exciting new idea that occurs while meditating by writing it down. There is no strict rule about whether or not to do this sometimes: personal integrity is valued above formulas. Instead, notice whether you habitually want to abandon meditation to pursue creativity or productivity that arises during your sit. It could be helpful to know that you *can* continue to meditate and let the creative thoughts come and go, before deciding to capture some of them.

Sleepiness

Sleepiness may include mental or physical fatigue, dullness, or torpor. If you are drowsy due to lack of sleep, it could be interesting to see if you can stay awake during your sit and find awareness nonetheless. It might also make better sense to catch up on sleep. Choose which you want to do, and fully embrace the experience.

Sleepiness can occur once you are sitting, even if you were wide awake beforehand and you're not underslept. Like thought stories, this kind of sleepiness is magnetizing. Staying aware at this point takes effort and determination. Notice the desire to move into oblivion, and the tension in the resistance.

When this kind of sleepiness intervenes, methods that maintain awareness within your sleepy situation are better than distraction-like antidotes. Sleepiness has arisen as an effect of meditation, so doing something different, such as splashing your face with cold water or getting up to drink coffee, defeats the purpose. Instead, see if you can maintain awareness while sleepiness does its thing, rather than trying to get rid of sleepiness.

Choose to stay awake and to sit with the discomfort that being awake entails. Bring awareness to the front of your face, to the light coming in below your eyelids. Notice how the regularity of your breathing pulls awareness towards sleepiness. Notice how the muscles in your eyelids are pulling awareness towards sleepiness.

> *It helps to bring awareness to your posture. Lengthen your spine. Find awareness in the space above and behind your head. If necessary, open your eyes and rest with a soft focus.*

Scaffolding methods that involve repetition, such as finding awareness in breathing or counting the breath, are less likely to work with sleepiness than others such as visualization or expanding sensory awareness. You can experiment to see what works this time.

You might find you can stay alert by alternating another meditation method with opening awareness. Song, walking meditation, and opening breath are all energizing meditation methods. Evolving Ground teaches these practices on courses, gatherings, and retreats.

RESTLESS AGITATION

Restlessness ranges from subtle emotional discomfort all the way to an unbearable urge to scream and run away. You may feel a desire to move, or to stop meditating and do something else.

Intense restlessness is most common during the first few months of opening awareness, but it can occur at any time for any meditator, no matter how experienced they are.

First, check there is no physical safety risk. It's usually obvious whether your restlessness results from the emotional constraint of sitting still or from physical pain.

Stay with the discomfort as long as you can without risking injury. Notice the texture and flavor of the discomfort. See if you can locate an associated sensation in your body. Breathe into the sensation, and notice the place that holds it.

Notice your accompanying attitude. Are you miserable, afraid, bored? Without criticism, see if you can bring a lightness of attitude to the situation. Be patient with your restlessness, without expecting it to ease or go away.

Bring awareness to psychological, emotional, or physical resistance to sitting. Often these are connected. Notice the conflict between the intention to sit and the desire to get up. Find awareness in the texture and sensation of the resistance to sitting.

When you get up at the end of your session, enjoy the sensation of moving. Appreciate having sat through the unpleasant experience and enjoy the contrast of free movement.

If you are regularly resistant, you may have lost sight of your reasons for meditating. Perhaps you wrote them down when I recommended that in the "Discovering your purpose" section of *How to practice?* It may be time to review that section, and your notes, now. It may be time to reconsider, if your former motivation seems stale. Recall times when meditation seemed satisfying. Why?

Boredom

Boredom is the biggest obstacle for many beginning meditators.

Thinking and feeling are often enjoyable and useful. Our path encourages both, as ways to creativity and to powerful, responsible effectiveness.

When left without external stimulation, it's common to use thoughts and emotions—even negative emotions—as entertainment. Inventing scenarios that generate exquisite or excruciating feelings is quite natural. Everybody does it. It is not good or bad.

During opening awareness meditation, however, we remain uninvolved with thoughts and emotions. Then we can see the process clearly, and choose not to fuel it for a while. Do not ignore, shut down, or cut off the entertainment-generation process. Notice it fully, without immersive involvement.

At first this choice may seem unappealing. It takes effort to remain uninvolved from personally meaningful stories. Notice how much less interesting the stories become as you remain aware of your process and cease feeding it. Their supposedly acute meaningfulness may dissipate.

Often we generate unnecessary emotional turbulence out of fear of such meaninglessness. Even painful emotional experiences may seem preferable, so in a panic, or unconsciously, we invent meaningfully awful scenarios to fill the empty space.

When the entertainment evaporates—what does that leave you with?

In its place, you may find boredom, quiet, nebulosity, or nothingness.

If you are not used to that, it can be terrifying.

Or, you may feel annoyed: "This is a huge waste of time, nothing is happening, I should be doing something useful!" You leap up from the meditation cushion and throw yourself into some supposedly valuable activity—to avoid perceiving how things are, without commentary. Your commitment to *doing*, to involvement with the world is meaningful and important—but can you remain uninvolved with the compulsion for a few minutes?

If all your thoughts are boring, that's a sign that they may soon disappear, because you aren't motivated to feed them. If you can rest in awareness without interesting content, you may find that the uninteresting content vanishes too.

Welcome boredom as the threshold of spacious clarity: vivid awareness without thought.

FRUSTRATION WITH SLOW PROGRESS

Frustration happens when you want your meditation to be going some way other than it is—faster, better, clearer, calmer. Notice that you want something different than what is happening. Acknowledge what actually *is* happening. Stay with it for a while. See if you can deliberately choose for *things to be how they are* right now, rather than how you want them to be.

Notice the desire for instant results. Appreciate this desire as fuel for continuity in your practice. Opening awareness may seem, at times, overwhelming, challenging, difficult, or simply too much responsibility.

Notice any attempt to push away or squash your irritation. When you notice the desire for things to be different, see also the associated desire to control circumstances.

Notice the texture and sensation of frustration as it characterizes your meditation. Welcome it. Appreciate it. Experiment with the application of more precision, channeling the energy of frustration into breath awareness, for example.

Alternatively, experiment with loosening the grip of frustration.

Relax, smile, feel the space around you.

Notice expectations that you hold, standards that you set for yourself. Where do they come from? What is behind them, what motivates them? What stands in the way of your dropping them while sitting?

"Policeman mind" is an attitude that attempts to make awareness happen all the time. It regards every moment as a potential failure or success. Policeman mind constantly asks "am I aware right now?" This obsessive vigilance obstructs spontaneous clarity. Allow the state to come and go, instead.

Splitting, burnout, and rebellion

Sometimes, if you really don't feel like it, a question arises whether to meditate or not. Forcing yourself into a daily habit, despite resistance, is a slog. The benefit of daily discipline is that you do get the hours in… and that makes the difference. The potential downside is that you will *split* yourself into a controlling, dominant meditator whose job is to overcome your other chaotic, unruly self. Your meditation practice may come to rely on the tight control of an authoritarian regime. This is a tenuous situation because it divides your experience into two parts in tension with each other—one dominant, one controlled. Your carefree, repressed part might eventually rebel, exploding the confines of your ideal world.

Here are some ways to establish familiarity with regularity that take into consideration the pitfalls of splitting, burnout, and rebellion.

> *Sometimes it's harder to start meditating than to stay once you are there.*

Creating a daily minimum timebox with a very low bar (two minutes, or five) is an effective way to establish a routine and to keep your options open. When you are establishing familiarity, you do not yet know how much you care about meditation. You can only find out by sitting. Promise yourself that you will sit for your minimum timebox, come what may. Keeping to your word makes it more powerful.

If circumstances allow, set up your meditation place so that it is ready and waiting for you. All you need to do is go to it and sit down.

If you notice restlessness or feel a strong urge to get up and move, don't worry; this is normal. You could acknowledge and include your restlessness in awareness, noticing any temptation to ignore or shut out the discomfort.

Sometimes, spend a little more time meditating than feels easily manageable. If you feel restless after five minutes, attempt opening awareness for six minutes. Build your capacity until you want to sit for thirty minutes fairly regularly. Extend beyond thirty minutes when your interest and circumstances allow. Sitting for an hour for the first time is deeply gratifying!

If you like to set goals, be kind to yourself by setting goals that you are confident you will achieve. Always keep your minimum sit duration to a length that seems easily manageable.

Scheduling your practice at the same time every day helps establish familiarity. Once you have a daily routine, the regularity provides momentum for you to carry out your intent to practice. If your life circumstances aren't conducive to sitting at a regular time, consider planning when you will sit a day or two ahead.

> *"One analogy that I find resonates for me is dirt settling out of still water in a glass. There are diminishing returns to increased duration of letting the dirt settle. There is also the slowly-changing limit at any given time of the stillness of the glass due to environmental vibrations.*
>
> *On any given day, duration may enable settling of the conceptual mind. There may also be a slowly-changing limit of how quiet the conceptual mind can become. Practicing very short duration (1 minute, 5 minute) opening awareness may not fully settle the conceptual mind but can still cumulatively increase the capability for settling the mind."*

—Ari, Evolving Ground apprentice

DISSOCIATION

Dissociation is a floaty state in which you feel untouchable, separate from your own and others' experience. It is usually calm, constant, and may be accompanied by a sense of the surreal or absurd. There is some sense that "you" are not the person engaged in the activity, that you are watching yourself from a distance, separated from the "you" that is going about responding to daily circumstances. The response to all things from a dissociated state is the same: detached indifference. You may feel perfect, untouchable, equanimous.

Others may feel upset and saddened by your dissociation. They may describe you as "out of reach" or "distant." Your dissociated experience sees them as "not getting it" and unnecessarily emotional.

Some meditation systems regard dissociation as a sign of progress, and use more positive-sounding vocabulary to describe the state: calm, equanimity, non-attachment. I use "dissociation" because it differentiates calmness, awareness, and spacious clarity from the state described above.

> *It is possible to remain calm while fully connected with experience, consciously aware of being, without becoming numb to sensory experience, and without separating your relational self from a detached, abstract observer-self.*

Dissociation is most likely to result from concentrative techniques that regard emotions as distractions. However, it can sometimes occur in opening awareness, especially if you have previously established a concentrative practice and are not used to the difference. If you experience dissociation, bring awareness into your body. Notice sensation, notice arising emotion, notice how the experience of your senses connects you with your environment. Practice any of the scaffolding exercises associated with physicality, embodiment, and awareness of the senses.

Dissociation impedes your capacity to feel a full range of emotions. It may feel effortless because the energetic cost is hidden. This is potentially dangerous. Like a pressure cooker about to explode, everything looks fine from the outside. However, dissociation can lead to:

- Acting out hidden desires in secret without admitting the internal conflict to yourself or others

- Resentment of aspects of yourself and of others

- Polarized, sudden extremes of expression, uncontrolled irritation, anger, or hatred

- Flatness, depression, loss of meaning

- Distancing/isolation/lack of empathy for loved ones

- Sameness in response to varied circumstances

Your body was made to feel. Opening awareness leads to vivid spacious clarity in ordinary activities through unobstructed awareness of embodied experience. Your senses are the doorways to relational, connected presence. Joyful creativity is freed when you give up using energy against yourself to suppress natural responsiveness.

Weird side effects

Many people spend most of their time immersed in thought stories and activities, vaguely and occasionally aware of the present moment. As conscious awareness increases through meditation, aspects of your being that you normally pass over become more apparent. This newly heightened awareness can momentarily distort perception so that odd experiences occur.

A typical, weird side effect early on in opening awareness is a falling sensation. You may feel dizzy, or experience a fizzy sensation in your heart center, a sense of groundlessness, like you are falling off the edge of a cliff—all while you know that you are unmoving, firmly seated. This rarely continues in the long term. Bring awareness into your body and notice your physical connection with the ground. Practice the scaffolding exercise *Finding awareness in sensation*.

Proprioceptive distortions are also common. Some people experience:

- A sense of their body becoming huge or miniscule

- Physical asymmetry: one arm seems longer than the other, or it seems as though the body is leaning over to one side

Changes in the field of vision or sound may include:

- High pitched ringing

- Visual anomalies, moving colors, dots, patterns

You can simply sit with odd experiences, without either prolonging or ignoring them. Notice the "texture" of the experience. Bringing awareness to your location in space highlights your relationship with the environment around you. The scaffolding exercise *Finding awareness in sounds and light* may be particularly useful here.

These odd happenings tend to characterize a phase of "getting used to" meditation. Sitting with heightened awareness, and decreased thought-immersion, is mentally, emotionally, and physiologically unusual. It takes a while to adjust, and can even be frightening. Eventually, familiarity with awareness supersedes its non-ordinariness, and the odd effects give way to prolonged, stable calm.

Some unusual experiences can be blissful. Waves of pleasurable sensation throughout the body, heightened sexual arousal, beautiful warmth and spacious opening in the gut, heart, throat, and head, and along the spine, are all fairly common. These tend to occur after establishing some stability in practice.

Some meditation systems regard effects like these as signs of achieving progressive stages. In opening awareness they may occur at any time and are not regarded as special. Ecstatic, blissful states are captivating, but they are not the point of this meditation path. Intentionally maintaining them, on or off the cushion, eventually leads to a distorted perception of how things are. It's tempting to constantly re-generate blissful experience, but if it becomes an obsession it can obstruct clear, responsive involvement with others.

Subtle, pleasurable kinesthetic sensation is a natural effect of opening awareness. You can be confident that it will arise naturally, without forcing, on and off the cushion, in response to circumstances.

Allow any unusual side-effects to come and go, maintaining awareness, neither encouraging nor discouraging them. Find awareness in the experience and let it last as long as it lasts, without intentionally prolonging or curtailing the sensation.

Emotional turbulence

Changing our relationships with emotions is what makes meditation so powerful for life. The ways we relate with our circumstances, with other people, with our projects—all may be limited by fixed, habitual emotional responses.

Experiencing emotions within spacious clarity gives freedom from compulsion. It opens up unbounded choices for action. This is a central aspect of the path for Evolving Ground.

Some other meditation systems regard emotions as the main hindrances to spiritual attainment. From that perspective, meditation is the process of subjugating, diminishing, or even eliminating them.

> *Opening awareness welcomes emotions. It leads to transforming emotional experiences, and its outcome is spacious, passionate involvement in life.*

When you can stay present with all emotions, you are no longer driven by the effort to control them lest they control you. In your day-to-day life, courage, curiosity, appreciation, joy, and graciousness become commonly available.

THERAPY AND OPENING AWARENESS

Some valuable results of opening awareness meditation resemble or complement those of psychotherapy—although their methods are quite different.

Many therapies facilitate self-confidence, based on conceptual, relational, and emotional understanding. Knowing yourself, your preferences, and your limits is important. Therapies may rely on narrative and commentary to clarify personal processes. From that, you can gain skill in working with turbulent emotions, which may have caused you trouble when they led to poor choices of action. Therapy may help you consolidate boundaries and identity, self-worth, agency and autonomous activity. These are prerequisite for emotionally mature relationships.

Depending on how you are now, you may want to practice self-confidence and self-worth in therapy before or while starting a meditation practice. If you have unprocessed trauma, difficulty dealing with your emotions or noticing and responding effectively to emotional pressure from others, therapy can be a valuable preparation or complement for opening awareness.

Unlike some therapies, opening awareness is not about consolidating boundaries and identity; nor does it use verbal understanding of emotional patterns, or seek to change them. It cannot and should not replace psychotherapy. Consider therapy if you want to build or reinforce a self-respecting identity, or want to learn reliable methods for avoiding emotionally-driven self-defeating actions.

Opening awareness can develop emotional and relational competence, but via a quite different route. It leads to another, complementary sort of confidence, based in a clear mind, free from commentary. Spacious clarity steps outside language to reveal how thinking and feeling *are*. This is quite different from the practice *of* talking, thinking, and reflecting in therapy. However, it too brings emotional and relational habits into view, thereby making more choices and self-possibilities available.

The self-confidence developed in therapy is based in a realistic, factual appraisal of your increasing ability to deal with challenging emotions and interactions. The confidence developed in opening awareness is recognition of the vivid open space that surrounds and underlies all emotions and interactions. It is unconditional, not reliant on facts or evidence reflecting your self, relationships, or life. It is confidence in being, not in your circumstances.

In everyday experience, this confident competence leads to fluid, spontaneously responsive activity.

WHEN EMOTIONS ARISE, WELCOME THEM

Meditating sometimes reveals hidden emotions, or stronger feelings than you had been aware of. In the short term, this may make your sitting practice more difficult. Turbulent emotions may seem like annoying distractions, and obstacles to the "real business" of meditation.

Opening awareness includes everything in experience—and particularly emotions. Learning to sit with emotions, without having to react to them, is perhaps the most valuable aspect of meditation. It is only when you experience emotions in spacious clarity that you can live congruently. It is better to find space for your feelings than to be mercilessly driven by them. This *is* the real business of meditation.

There is no need to go looking for emotions. Opening awareness provides the space for your thoughts to quiet. Sitting still with an open, alert attitude is a natural invitation to feel. Let emotions come and go, respecting their movement in the space of awareness, without involvement.

When you provide a space bigger than your emotions in which they are free to move, they cannot control you. Attending to the space in which they occur, rather than perpetuating the patterns that constrain them, it becomes evident that you contain—you are larger than—your emotions. You have them; they do not have you.

Working with emotions in opening awareness has two aspects: remaining conceptually uninvolved, and maintaining a clear sensory awareness that includes everything you experience.

> *Notice the narrative, see how it functions, and find the sensation.*

Remain uninvolved with emotionally charged thoughts

Emotions and emotionally charged thinking feed each other. Emotional intensity can make thoughts especially compelling. Fear, anger, hope, and desire provoke imaginary scenarios. It's difficult to stop yourself rehearsing past or future events, visualized or narrated, and planning actions you might take in response.

The method here is the same as in all opening awareness: remain uninvolved. Refrain from engaging with the relentless, repetitive narratives. Refrain from feeding thoughts. Allow them, do not suppress them, but do not encourage them. If raccoons wander through your back yard, you don't need to scare them off, but you don't need to put out a bowl of milk for them either. You can just watch and appreciate them until they wander off again.

Notice any desire to judge yourself or your experience. Refrain and return to opening awareness.

> *Notice that what is happening now is different from the projected, imagined scenarios.*

Notice the vividness of the troubling stuff that arises in your mind. Appreciate the mind's endless, infinite capacity for creativity. Those events are not happening *now*. Bring awareness to your present situation, location, and position. Remain in the present. Appreciate the present moment.

Emotions, and the thoughts that accompany them, can seem intensely meaningful. Their meaningfulness may seem to compel obsessive replay. It helps to recognize how changeable they are, like weather. Sunny days pass; storms pass. You may like one better than the other, but with experience in meditation, you find that usually neither lasts long—often less long than a single meditation session.

Emotions often dissipate in meditation. This may be a great relief. Half an hour in, you forget you were angry, and find yourself enjoying the sound of the rain on the roof instead. Somehow, whatever you were angry about no longer seems particularly meaningful. That may be a relief… or it might be annoying, if you were *enjoying* being mad. Notice how justification perpetuates anger. What is it like to remain uninvolved with the thought stream without cutting off from sensation in your body?

Emotions may also persist, and even intensify, if you remain uninvolved with related thoughts—as we'll see later in this chapter.

Feel emotions as bodily energy and sensations

Maintaining clear awareness of emotions means feeling their details accurately, without conceptual analysis.

Include everything. Suppress, ignore, exaggerate, or intensify nothing.

When an emotion arises, notice its texture. What makes it distinct? In particular, find the bodily sensation associated with it. Notice where you are holding tension. For example, angry thoughts are commonly accompanied by heat and pressure in the chest, tension in the chin, or forehead pain. Notice other physical sensations, such as nausea—often connected with fear—or a tight throat, common with sadness.

Stay with the sensation without looking for change, hoping for change, or trying to make change happen. Try not to analyze the sensation; simply stay with it. Notice how the feeling colors your experience. Notice what else is happening: other sensations in your body, and sounds around you. Notice any restriction in your breathing, and breathe deeply into your torso.

Bring awareness to your whole body, and your connection with the ground. Feel the solidity of the earth underneath you, the reliability of the gravitational pull to the ground. Make sure that you are fully conscious of your torso, butt, and legs.

Opening awareness is not about retreating into headspace. If you notice that your spatial awareness is mostly confined to headspace, expand awareness throughout your body, and beyond.

Feel the open space around your body, and the open space around the emotion in your awareness. No matter how intense the emotion, it is not the whole of your experience.

As you leave any meditation session, notice changes in sensation.

Notice any inclination to close down emotional sensations, or to put them to one side.

As you go about your daily activities, discover the possibility of fully engaging with life circumstances, doing what needs to be done, without either shutting down or firing up emotions.

Expanding your emotional range

Most of us allow ourselves only an unnaturally constricted range of emotions. Some, that we feel justified in, we artificially amp up. We turn the volume down on others, ones for which we feel shame or fear.

We may limit our emotions to a few preferred ones, replaying them again and again in different scenarios, involving others in their intensity. Meditation reveals patterns of upset, anger, justification, and drama. These may hide sadness and loneliness. We perceive our actual feelings only through a fog of moralizing self-judgments, self-justifications, and elaborate rules of appropriateness.

We may deliberately refuse to experience other emotions. Some we don't want to admit ever having felt at all; we hide them from plain sight, and may forget what they were like. Our experience may have been that these emotions caused us to say and do things we were punished for, or that we later regret. We may have experienced "out of control" emotions rampaging through our psyches, wrecking the fragile internal harmony we built by balancing divergent desires. Or, we fear that "having a meltdown" could leave us unable to function normally, perhaps for days, until we regain composure. We worry about what intense feelings would mean for our self-understanding: implications for how we should see ourselves. "Feeling that way would mean I am an angry/timorous/greedy person, which is a bad thing to be."

Such fears may be partly realistic. However, they are mainly based on experiences from childhood, when accurate emotional sensitivity and wise, selective expression are infeasible. In overly permissive environments, some children learn to get their way with exaggerated acting-out of deliberately-intensified negative emotions. For other children, self-control may be possible only by bashing emotions with a blunt object until they stop moving, and then hiding them at the back of the closet. As adults, we have better choices.

Meditation methods—opening awareness among others—can train accurate emotional perception; can free us from the compulsion to act on emotions; and can liberate responsible, beneficial emotional expression.

Holding and enjoying intense emotions

In opening awareness, you commit to sitting with emotions without acting on them externally. By remaining uninvolved, you choose not to respond to them internally, either.

Remaining uninvolved means not doing "aboutness." You find that you don't have to have thoughts about emotions. You don't have to have emotions about thoughts. You don't have to have emotions about emotions, either. You can just let them be as they are, remaining present as they come and go.

You may have been using thoughts to intensify or replay upsetting emotions, because you fear you may become unseen or unheard without them. Remaining uninvolved with the thoughts provides space in which they will lose their hold.

Alternatively, by remaining present with feelings, opening awareness may intensify emotions if you've been ignoring them; or if you have been using thoughts to suppress or diminish emotions because you sense they may become overwhelming if allowed their natural dynamism.

With practice, you will gradually gain confidence that you need not be dominated by habitual emotions; and that you can fully experience maximally intense ones without negative consequences. Then you know from experience that, when you leave emotions alone without compulsive internal responses, they cannot harm your mind. You find that the intensity is not only tolerable, it becomes *enjoyable*—even in the case of supposedly "negative" emotions like anger and fear.

Learning how to tolerate and enjoy strong emotions in the safe environment of meditation is practice for doing the same in difficult interpersonal situations. Meditation is training in courage. When you know you don't have to act as your emotions suggest, you can have confidence in taking constructive actions instead.

Knowing that you don't have to react to your own emotions, you can have confidence that you won't be compelled by other people's emotions either. You don't have to have emotions about other people's emotions—just as you don't have to have emotions about your own emotions. You can appreciate others' emotions, like your own, as expressions of biological energy. You notice when you have ascribed unnecessary additional meanings ("they are angry, that must mean I did something bad, so I am a bad person"). You can act without having to preemptively defend your self against the feelings you worry others may have.

Confidence in emotional capacity liberates you for powerful, playful, creative, helpful interaction.

Gaining this confidence is hard work. It may take many months, perhaps several years, to experience the full range of emotions in meditation—especially if you are used to crowding them out, or preferring some over others.

Fear of intense emotions can be a bigger obstacle in meditation than the emotions themselves. However unwanted or painful an emotion, welcome it. It cannot harm awareness. Discovering this dissolves fear. Sit with the physical sensation of the emotion and allow it to be as it is. Sensation is likely to change in some way. It may intensify or dissipate. Whatever happens, let it happen.

This can be difficult; even terrifying at times. Take it slowly, talk with friends, and find support.

In opening awareness practice, one remains silent and still. Particularly intense emotions may make that temporarily impossible. If you are used to bottling up your emotions and are unfamiliar with expressing them, it may be better to sound them non-verbally while continuing to meditate, than to abandon your session. If you need to cry, cry—without prolonging crying beyond its natural length. If you need to yell, yell, once, without dramatizing it. You do not need to make a habit of this.

If an emotion becomes altogether too much to bear, take a break. Be patient. It can take a while to find the vast, spacious clarity in which all emotions can simply be themselves without threatening to engulf you. Always be ready to stop temporarily and come back later, if acquainting yourself with your spectrum of emotional response is overwhelming.

Although generally different emotions come and go, you may find that something has become "stuck." This could show up as persistent depression, covered in a separate section later. Or, it could be recurrent emotional pain, in response to traumatic memories or circumstances.

Semi-deliberately intensifying emotional pain may be a habitual response. Sometimes we think we *ought* to feel pain, perhaps as punishment for a past transgression we regret. Or maybe we consider our-selves *justified* in feeling it. Notice such thoughts. Or, perhaps we once had such thoughts, but have forgotten our reasons, and emotional pain is just a deeply ingrained habit now.

If you are used to intensifying pain, meditation may provide space in which to loosen the agonizing knot. Notice any desire to prolong or to re-ignite the experience of pain, particularly re-living the same trauma pattern again and again. Pain is intensely meaningful. Some-times it gets trapped by the meaning you ascribe to it. Notice how sto-ries perpetuate pain, protracting it with repetition, inviting immersion. If you can experience how the narrative works, rather than what it says, it may lose its power over your emotional process. See if you can find, and stay aware of, any associated sensation in your body. Try not to judge yourself or the story as good or bad. This is one of the hardest experiences to deal with in meditation. But getting to see how your narrative patterns capture and direct your experience is a superpower!

If you are traumatized or experiencing acute emotional pain, don't rely solely on this brief discussion to guide your meditation. Find other practitioners to talk with and to help you decide what is the best way for-ward. If trauma is seriously detrimental for your life and relationships with others, seek professional help. You may find that first spending time in therapy or with other healing practices might be a better fit for you for now.

Clarifying hidden, mixed, and subtle emotions

Having spent your entire life generating thoughts and emotions about emotions, and thoughts and emotions about *those* thoughts and emotions, the feelings themselves may be buried deep under layers of commentary. When at times they emerge, they are encrusted with your past reactions to them: like statues recovered from an ancient shipwreck, covered in corals and starfish and seaweed. You can make out only general, threatening shapes; the details are hidden.

When you remain uninvolved, the obscurations gradually drop off—without deliberate effort, and with no attempt at psychological analysis.

Emotions return to their natural, unadorned forms. Now you can see them clearly in the space of awareness. Separated from their supposed meanings, they are revealed as transparent and brilliantly colored, like oversized gummy bears. This includes the dramatically-posed, supposedly negative emotions like anger, fear, lust, and greed. They are chewy but edible: you can enjoy their intense, distinctive flavors for their own sake.

Through remaining uninvolved, you can expect to discover emotions you hid from yourself long ago. If you meditate consistently and long enough, you will eventually experience all human qualities within yourself. Your spacious clarity holds all kinds of surprises—you are both monster and angel and all the possibilities in between. None of these rigidly define you.

Sometimes you will find yourself unexpectedly feeling two emotions at once—even seemingly contradictory ones. As you come to perceive emotions more clearly, you will discover subtle shades of feeling for which there are no words.

Habitual emotional responses to emotions can conceal the original feeling—sometimes several layers deep.

Anger is a common response to fear: if you feel threatened by someone, you may want to hurt them or control them. If fear is unacceptable, because as a child you interpreted it as weakness for example, then you may only feel the anger. You do not allow yourself fear... then you may be perpetually angry, which is not an enjoyable or helpful way to be.

Sitting with anger, remain uninvolved with the furious ruminations and recriminations and fantasies of revenge. Notice where you are holding tension—in your chest or jaw, perhaps—and find space around it. Without involvement, and as physical tension releases, fear may reveal itself.

When fear shows up in meditation, it may be accompanied by narratives of invisibility, loneliness, or rejection; of financial or relational inadequacy or loss; of illness or death. Those may be hard to sit with. Trust that by leaving the narratives alone, the fear itself will eventually become bearable. You may come to greet it as a familiar acquaintance dropping by for a visit.

In its most nebulous form, fear may be connected to loss of certainty, security, or familiarity. Experiencing such abstract, *existential* fear while sitting is a great opportunity. There is no specific threat, so you can identify and appreciate fear just as it is, without distracting stories. Notice whether you subtly label this sensation of fear as negative. If so, see if it is possible to experience the sensation without judgment.

This groundlessness, this sense of falling helplessly, is closely related to spacious clarity—and may flip into it.

Fear often obscures sadness.

Every one of us has *already* experienced losses in life. Sadness is a natural response. It may be experienced as negative and unwanted, though. Fear is fear of possible future losses, but also fear of how we will feel if they come to pass. If sadness is unacceptable, every fear is doubled: accompanied by the extra fear of sadness.

Sadness takes time.

Anger is a quick emotion: it can come and go in a minute, and you are done with it. Sadness is slow. Feeling a loss fully takes time and space and presence; sometimes weeks, months, or even years. During that time, you may have less room for other things.

It's natural to busy yourself with *getting stuff done.* This is a reasonable coping strategy. However, it is easy to bury your sadness under activity.

Opening awareness is an opportunity to experience old losses fully—if that is what naturally arises. You are sitting without an agenda anyway. You are deliberately setting aside whatever busy thinking you might otherwise do. There is time enough for sadness.

As you breathe out, voice your sadness in the sound "Aaah." Notice any arising sensation.

There is nothing to do except to be with the feeling, remaining uninvolved with memories and regrets if they arise. You may find sadness cool and clear like a mountain stream, in contrast with the heat of anger and the murk of fear.

Sadness is quite unlike depression. It's common to confuse them, because depression is commonly a strategy for dealing with sadness when it seems overwhelming. (There's more about that in the depression section later in this chapter.) Depression makes you feel dead. You don't care about anything except wishing for the pain to lift. Depression seems like it will go on forever, though.

Sadness, unlike depression, feels alive. And, in the space around it, you feel glad to be alive, despite your loss. To fully experience sadness is an expression of care. You care about the loss—you embrace and recognize its meaning for yourself and others. When you have worked through sadness, often you find what remains is joy in living.

Basic okayness and unconditional security

Basic okayness is a ground in experience that gives rise to an attitude. It is the felt sense that there is nothing fundamentally wrong with you, and nothing intrinsically wrong with the world. Basic okayness comes from a shift in the timbre of being, not from analysis or evidence.

Basic okayness is the opposite of an attitude that many cultures inculcate—particularly ones influenced by renunciative religions. That is the belief that you're fundamentally *bad* in some way, that the world is somehow intrinsically defective, and that these are huge problems. This promotes attitudes of personal worthlessness, self-denial, and revulsion for the world. It leads to muddied perception, shutting out vividness; and helplessness: inability to act, due to self-doubt and lack of trust that change is realistic.

Basic okayness simply experiences being in the world as fundamentally fine. Mundane reality is workable and interesting and engaging and exciting, and so are you.

You discover basic okayness by *remaining uninvolved* with the anti-life morality, anti-self psychological explanations, and anti-world spiritual narratives we've all been fed. In time, in opening awareness, those thoughts and the accompanying feelings drop away. All that crud has been obscuring the fact that basic okayness is not something you have to generate. It was always already there, unnoticed. You are naturally engaged, appreciative, and ready for whatever presents itself.

Basic okayness is accompanied by the felt sense of unconditional security.

Pragmatic, relative security is sensible to pursue, to a reasonable extent, through prudent actions that create favorable conditions. Relative security is never fully stable, though. Absolute factual security is impossible. Conditions may change unpredictably. Disaster is always possible. You may die at any moment.

Unconditional security comes from connection with the felt sense of basic okayness. You can trust that, whatever happens, you will remain present and connected, and you will respond accurately to what you perceive. You will be available in unexpected breakdowns, and for surprising opportunities that defy familiar definitions—rather than reacting based on habitual patterns or expectations. You will act on the basis of current perceptions, rather than retreating into sterile analysis or unrealistic fantasies. You will fully experience your feelings in the face of trouble, but you won't be driven into ill-considered actions by overwhelming emotional reactions. You will do your best. You are not paralyzed because you feel fundamentally inadequate.

Unconditional security can't guarantee a good outcome, but it means your attitude remains impeccable. If you are about to die, and there is no way to escape, that is in a sense fine. It is what is happening *now*; it is what is real. There is no point wringing your hands or imagining unavailable alternatives. You can meet death with dignity and enthusiasm.

Radiating liberated energy

Unwanted, "negative" emotions often show up as challenges for beginning meditators. You will eventually encounter "positive" emotions in meditation too: contentment, wonder, awe, good cheer, bliss, and joy.

Those may come a bit later, perhaps unexpectedly, perhaps as a shock. You may have suppressed or diminished your positive emotions, the same way you did negative ones. You may have forgotten what they feel like at full volume. You may believe that you don't *deserve* to feel that good. You may fear that experiencing such enjoyment could lead you to irresponsibility, or addiction, or others' disapproval. Positive emotions in meditation rarely cause such problems. Occasionally, they may temporarily hinder your practice because they are so overwhelming they seem intolerable.

In any case, however mild or earth-shattering, opening awareness treats positive emotions just like every other experience: you include them and remain uninvolved. Remaining uninvolved is the antidote to compulsion.

By treating all emotions the same way, the distinction between "negative" and "positive" may blur or even vanish. All emotions are equally sensations without intrinsic meanings. Freed from their narratives, you may find yourself enjoying the sensations behind desire, anger, fear, and sadness—and you may find positive applications for them in everyday life. Liberated from fixed interpretations, they engender play, effectiveness, creativity, spontaneity, and responsibility.

> *Joy is always available to everyone, but is often hidden behind fear, anger, frustration, anxiety, or depression.*

Joy is the natural response to freedom of feeling. With consistent, long-term regular practice, opening awareness commonly uncovers joy.

Joy is socially and culturally constricted. It is mistakenly pitted against systematicity, rationality, and predictability. Sourceless, boundless joy seems threateningly irresponsible! Joy may be the enemy of mindless routine, but suppressing it is a blunder of monumental proportions. Excited, joyous teams have accomplished some of the most socially valuable advances.

Notice how others respond to your joy. Notice how infectious and enlivening your joyous expression is. Notice how, when you authentically express joy, you smile, and others do too. Joy that arises naturally in your meditation carries over into life circumstances. It brings energy and motivation to all sorts of activities, especially group involvement.

Engaged practice is enjoyable, involved activity with others, in the real world, to make cool, beautiful, useful stuff. Evolving Ground organizes groups for exploring spacious emotional response in everyday circumstances. We charge practice with additional methods that—unlike opening awareness—*engage* strong emotions constructively.

ENERGY TROUBLES: DEPRESSION AND OVEREXCITEMENT

Depression and hypomania (overexcitement) are not emotions. I discuss them in this chapter because they are conditions in which you relate to emotions dysfunctionally.

Depression

Depression is not an emotion. It is the condition of refusing to experience emotions. You shut them down because they seem too painful and difficult to deal with.

You shut down perception, because it provokes feelings. You withdraw from activities and relationships, because they involve emotions. You find yourself unable—or, perhaps more accurately, unwilling—to engage with anything. This may be temporarily intelligent, when intense negative emotions threaten real harm to your psyche.

It is a bad longer-term strategy. If you are feeling so low and unmotivated that you have stopped taking care of yourself and any movement seems like too much effort, ask someone to help you get medical advice. Many people who experience periods of serious depression get better with support, and go on to enjoy life. Although in this section I'll explain depression as something you *choose*, it can have involuntary biological causes as well, which are best treated some other way.

Opening awareness meditation may be counterproductive for depression. Depression is *refusal to become involved*—and opening awareness is *choosing to remain uninvolved*. Remaining uninvolved is best practiced when there is much that awareness *could* become involved with, and the pull toward thinking, feeling, and acting runs strong.

When everything feels numb, bleak, and gray, the first step is to reawaken the natural capacity for involvement. There are many ways to do that. Often effective are physical exercise, walks in natural beauty, appreciating music or art, and taking on projects on behalf of other people. There are also practices other than opening awareness that actively encourage involvement.

It seems like depression comes upon you and that there's nothing you can do about it. You don't notice the effort required to distance yourself from all the feelings. You are numb to the pain and the pleasure of life, and the numbness obscures the force of the energy you are using to keep it that way.

Shutdown *feels* passive... but something is doing the shutting down. It's you. Noticing the slow thoughts and attenuated feelings that arise when meditating with depression may reveal the machinery of suppression—and then you may choose to dismantle it.

The way out of depression is involvement.

With some modification, in some cases, opening awareness can be helpful in depression. Because perception is always present, vividness is available even in depression—if you are willing. You could try spending your meditation session *fully involved* in your senses.

Keep your eyes open. Notice the texture of your surroundings. See if you can enjoy sounds and colors for their own sake. Find something to smell.

Bring awareness to your body. Sensation is always present. Find it. You can also awaken physical sensation with movement and exercise. Try the walking awareness practice, described in the *Scaffolding practices* chapter.

The way out of depression is relaxation.

Notice where you are holding tension in your body and see if you can release it. Do you notice an accompanying tension in your mind, in relation to the past or the future?

See if you can release the past and the future from the present moment. Just be.

The way out of depression is appreciation.

Depression is a response to overwhelm, so a different option is to hone in on detail. Spend your meditation session noticing distinctions in your environment.

Especially, notice the quality of light and how textures change in the light. Bring appreciation of distinctions into your daily experience off the cushion.

Meditating with depression is courageous. It requires honesty. You are making a choice to bring alert curiosity to your experience even when that's the last thing you feel like doing.

It's likely that the first emotions to arise out of depression will be sadness and pain. You know this—and that is why you keep the depression going.

With relaxation, courage, and appreciation, you can open to the possibility. With experience meditating, you gain increasing confidence that you *can* withstand intense, unwanted feelings. You will embrace, and not reject, whichever sensation or emotion arises.

It could help to say to yourself: "Whatever happens, *may* it happen!"

You may be surprised by which emotions you encounter as you swim up out of depression. You may find yourself laughing and crying at the same time.

Hypomania: overexcitement

Hypomania is the mirror image of depression: a high energy state that distorts perception, and therefore action.

Opening to a wider, vaster experience in meditation is exciting. It quite often raises energy, physically and emotionally! Most of us have habitually narrowed our range of perception and expression. Finding a new capacity to move beyond habitual constraints makes you feel free and alive. Then a move in the direction of hypomania is natural, and usually not a problem.

Hypomania is excitement that *is* a problem. It can feel good, often euphoric, at the time. However, it can have bad interpersonal and practical consequences. You're speeding, your mind is racing, you are not thinking clearly. You may come across as grandiose, disinhibited, unrealistic in your assessments. You may talk faster than usual and monopolize conversation. Intense, incongruous emotions come and go suddenly. You might have a distorted perception of risk and do things you later regret.

Hypomania ranges from mild to extreme. It is on a continuum with clinical mania, which may require emergency intervention.

It's unusual for opening awareness to lead directly to hypomania, much less mania. Rarely, it can happen, especially if you have a biological predisposition to a bipolar condition.

> *If you know you are prone to excited, hypomanic states, you can look out for familiar warning signs, such as changes in your sleeping pattern, appetite, and behavior.*

If you have never experienced hypomania before, it may be frightening or disorienting. There are ways you can intervene to lower your energetic state:

- Close your eyes, slow your breathing, lower your head, or lie down

- Go to bed at night at a set time, to establish a routine, even if you don't feel tired

- Avoid alcohol and stimulants

- Turn off bright lights

- Leave busy environments; find somewhere quiet and calm

- Avoid high energy activities

If none of these work and you are afraid that hypomania is going to cause you or someone else harm, get professional help.

EIGHT

Spacious involvement in life

This book so far has been about opening awareness, which is *remaining uninvolved*. And yet, the *How to Practice* chapter led with:

> The overall aim of the path is passionate engagement with the fullness of life. That is the opposite of uninvolvement! However, opening awareness leads to spacious clarity, within which we perceive all of life with new, more vivid accuracy. We can find that spacious clarity in every other activity. Opening awareness trains us, through remaining temporarily uninvolved during practice sessions, to find clarity even while fully involved.

Meditation is fascinating and enjoyable for its own sake, but I value it most highly as a power-up for life. Opening awareness is the foundation for *spacious involvement*, which is a core training module in the Evolving Ground path.

The *Evolving Ground Fundamentals* journey walks that path. It is a route to finding freedom in relationship and responsible effectiveness in action. It has nine parts. *Opening awareness* is its first and foundational method.

I'd like to give a sense of how you might engage personally with this path. What that might look like in practice, and how it might transform your way of being, is highly individual. That depends on your goals and circumstances. The path does not prescribe any specific changes, or advocate any particular values.

The rest of this chapter summarizes the path, so that you can see how opening awareness becomes the foundation for more effective communication and action in life.

AWARENESS IN INTERACTIONS

In meditation, you gain new insight into how you are in interaction, and why. That gives you the basis for freedom to change.

In opening awareness, lacking interactive stimulation, your mind replays memories of emotionally meaningful interactions. It fantasizes variations of them. You imagine past or future events involving you, partly by recycling remembered conversations, relationships, and stories. Remaining aware of the thoughts, feelings, and sensations, but uninvolved with their implications, you notice *patterns*. These patterns are your strategies for relating.

Imaginative inventions of circumstances are personally meaningful, and typically their meaning is what you take to be important. As you learn to see fantasies more clearly, the purposes they serve come to seem more relevant than their content. You notice how they support your way of being in the world. Perhaps they are there to help you feel good. Sometimes they just make you feel bad. Either way, they're usually reassuringly familiar, and affirm how you perceive yourself and others.

It becomes increasingly difficult to take these imaginations seriously as you gain experience with opening awareness. That makes meditation easier: you are less likely to lose awareness in thought stories or emotional fantasies if they appear as self-perpetuating patterns, rather than absorbing realities. This is *spaciousness*: a wider view that is friendly, beneficent, yet unmoved. That is nothing like spaciness—the inability to focus, or to think clearly.

The familiar patterns of thoughts and feelings discovered in meditation also show up in your real-life interactions. Even while in real interactions, it's common to be so engrossed in imagined scenarios that you fail to notice that they reflect imperfectly how things are. Your interpretations of unfolding events conform to stale patterns, not reality. Yet they tell you how to be.

Now, you see clearly some familiar scripts you like to play. Perhaps you identify how and when they're most likely to kick in, or even the circumstances which led you to creating them.

You discover the interactive ways of being that you have created to meet your circumstances: heroic, magnificent, perhaps sometimes dark, sad, or lonely—always delightfully creative. *You* contain multitudes. Perceiving your response to life as transparent patterns rather than solid realities, you discover a lightness in being.

"Involvement" means you are there in the action, connected to what is happening, its salient details, and implications. At first you may be powerless to respond differently. Your interactions speed along as though on self-drive with automated momentum.

Seeing clearly the workings of your interactive mechanisms, one day you find the steering wheel. You can put your foot on the brakes, take a different route, even drive off-road into unexplored territory.

Spacious involvement is a way of being in the world, liberated from fixed patterns by awareness of them. Seeing them play out in life opens the possibility for new, more accurate responses. Sometimes those responses arise naturally in spacious involvement. Other methods that engage with emotions, energy, appreciation, sensations, and communication can help as well.

COMMUNICATING WITH INTEGRITY

Acting on established scripts lacks the awareness that enables you to take responsibility for results. When involvement loses awareness, following along old tracks of interaction, it becomes harder to act with spaciousness, choice, and integrity.

Spacious clarity, found in meditation, gives rise to awareness of the patterns of *pressure and expectation* in interactive situations. Seeing them clearly, you are no longer bound by them. Instead, you find the courage to speak in tune with your perception of how things are.

You can communicate without fear of how others might perceive you—or of how you might perceive yourself, if it doesn't go well. If necessary, you're willing to behave and communicate contrary to expectations, even when that risks alienation from your group. This does not make you a psychopath. It makes you an individual with integrity, involved in groups and relationships by choice rather than by conformity.

As you develop personal integrity in communicating from perception, you become reliable in a new way: you are accountable to your principles, not to others' feelings and opinions. You do what you said you would, what you can see is right, even when that disappoints your friends.

The more you see your own strategies, the more you see others'. Spaciousness makes it impossible to manipulate you. There is nothing to grab onto, nothing to push or pull. When someone tries to force an emotional response from you, you remain both uninvolved with their attempt and fully present—engaged with the person. You can be friendly and communicating and connected and unimpressed with their ploy.

Remaining uninvolved with a fixed idea about who you are, and how you have to be, frees you from the conceptual limitations of identity. You see through fantasies of attaining personal perfection. You are not a single, unified, fixed self. You are complex in your unbounded, undiscovered potential.

Spontaneous action

Spontaneous action breaks out of stuck patterns.

Opening awareness frees you from domination by your own mental contents: your thoughts, emotions, interpretations, habits, beliefs, desires, intentions, identities, and all of that other *stuff*. Those perpetuate patterns because they are experienced as opaque and static. They are also often somewhat abstract, and mostly concern matters elsewhere and elsewhen. They are much less relevant to what is happening *now* than they try to claim.

Having learned in opening awareness to remain uninvolved, you need not act on the basis of your mental contents. It is not that you are separated from them, or that they have vanished; it is that they have lost their power to compel.

Spontaneous action arises naturally from spacious involvement. Spaciousness frees you to act instead from fresh, panoramic perception of what is happening and what is becoming possible. Perception, by contrast with mental contents, is transient, transparent, always specific, always here and now. Every moment is new, and so can invite a unique, spontaneous interaction. Then you are no longer performing a script; perception is liberated from fixed patterns.

Spontaneous action is not something you can *decide to do*. It's spontaneous: it just *happens* from perceiving an unexpected possibility.

Spontaneous action is precise in response to accurate perception of a situation. It is effective, not irrational; responsible, not random; considerate, not heedless; empathic, not selfish; mature, not impulsive; realistic, not based on holistic fantasies.

Spaciousness and spontaneity do not imply abandoning conceptual thought, rationality, or planning. They imply using those when they are helpful, with intelligence and integrity. In many situations, it is good to think through consequences before acting. In others, such as a conversation, planning ahead what you will say is more often unhelpful. Your plan obscures your perception of other participants' unexpected responses. We fix others' patterns in our interpretations to the extent that we remain stuck in our own.

EMOTIONAL AND ETHICAL MATURITY

The practices discussed in this book's chapter *Emotional Turbulence* result in emotional maturity. That means perceiving all your emotions clearly, and not getting pushed by them into unwise actions. It means not dumping your emotions on other people, and not trying to manipulate them into feeling the emotions you want them to feel.

Remaining uninvolved with emotions enables you to relate effectively. That's not because you have become an emotionless robot or callous sociopath, but because you are not dominated by transient feelings—your own, or those of others you interact with. You perceive them accurately as dynamic aspects of the situation as a whole, and take them into account without automatically giving them priority.

Emotional maturity is a prerequisite to ethical maturity. No longer subject to every fleeting feeling, having stabilized the sense that you are basically okay, you can trust yourself not to be unduly selfish. You can trust yourself not to get pushed into morally dubious actions by others' expectations.

You have gained insight into how you are, and how you operate in interactions, through meditation. After a thousand hours of opening awareness, you will have seen the range of thoughts your mind is capable of. You will know your personal impulses, strategies, and copes. You can regard them with good humor and let them alone. You know what you might do—and you know what you won't.

Seeing clearly opens possibilities for a freer way of being. You may surprise yourself with spontaneous gestures of natural kindness and gracious play. Beneficence is a natural effect of stabilizing unconditional security.

> *When you no longer feel emotionally threatened, you are freed to desire others' happiness, and to act to further it.*

You can find this beneficence even in tense and difficult interpersonal interactions. Your spaciousness extends to appreciation and consideration for everyone, making room even for apparent adversaries.

Ethical maturity includes the recognition that no rules, principles, framework, formula, or ideology can reliably prescribe right action in specific situations. They are abstract, but *what is happening* is concrete. Every situation is unique and unboundedly complex, and so cannot be captured by prescribed patterns.

This means you cannot delegate personal responsibility to any moral theory. You take personal responsibility for moral choices. All ethical theorizing is relevant *sometimes*; you can take them into account when they are useful, without them governing you. You also cannot delegate moral choice to anyone else.

Your capability to remain uninvolved with theoretical ethical concepts, and to act on how you perceive the situation instead, enables mature moral choice. That does not guarantee good outcomes—but neither can anything else. Blamelessness is impossible; moral certainty is impossible. Life is messy and unpredictable. You will make mistakes sometimes, and you accept that, as an aspect of basic okayness. You are not paralyzed by moral uncertainty.

This is not equivalent to saying you feel free to do as you please, re-gardless of harm. On the contrary: freed from other's expectations, and from your own judgemental commentary, you can act autonomously for the benefit of all involved, with verve, flair, and an open heart.

LEADING

To be fully involved in life, you constantly update and expand your pat-terns of interaction according to context—not by taking on new expec-tations, but by discovering and expressing new capabilities. You step into larger worlds as a more spacious, more involved person.

Spacious involvement naturally gives rise to an attitude: you are willing to take active responsibility for how things are, and what might happen. You can read the broader context for its potential for change. You look for positive longer-term possibilities. When you can see what needs to be done, you act on that insight. Freed from the expectations and pressures of fixed interactive patterns, you take initiative, and re-sponsibility for the outcome.

The more your spacious involvement expands into unforeseen pos-sibilities, the more others naturally see you as a leader. This may mean stepping into a role when previously you may have lacked the courage. It could involve inventing a new role simply by doing and being what's needed. Or it may mean disregarding the limitations of clearly defined roles.

That doesn't mean that you take on more than you can reasonably expect to accomplish. It means you interact with integrity, confident in your capacity to listen and hear clearly, to support and encourage, to facilitate, choose, and direct.

Leading requires courage. It requires acknowledging discomfort, and recognizing the dangers of authority and power. Your courage is enabled by realistic trust in your own reliability. That trust is based in awareness in interactions, emotional and ethical maturity, integrity, and willingness to step into the unknown.

> *Skillful perception, creative choice, and confident action*
> *have become hallmarks of your way of being.*

Transitioning from other meditation paths

The method of opening awareness is distinct from that of many other meditation systems. Typically, they involve concentrated mental focus. Often, they aim for detachment, an experience of no-self, sometimes cessation of sensations altogether. The earlier chapter *What Makes Opening Awareness Different* explained how some of these differences stem from those methods' roots in renunciative spiritual systems. Opening awareness aims instead for a relaxed, spacious clarity, with no specific focus, fully including all of your self and your environment.

Many people come to opening awareness having already practiced meditation methods from renunciative paths. This chapter discusses that kind of transition broadly, glossing over differences in details of approach that might be appropriate depending on which specific system you have experience with.

The discussion here may be useful even without experience, because ideas in current popular culture about what meditation is mainly come from the vipassana tradition. They are misleading when applied to opening awareness. Recognizing what opening awareness *isn't* may help pin it down when it seems frustratingly vague. For example, opening awareness *doesn't* involve labeling, noting, concentration, focus on an object, observation, ignoring distractions, or non-attachment.

Although experience with other systems can make opening awareness harder in some ways, it gives you a head start in others. You have already learned to sit quietly and comfortably for significant periods, and you know what it is like to persist in remaining with a difficult practice in the face of the constant tug of thought-stories. Those are the major challenges for beginners who have no meditation experience at all.

Meditation

Renunciative methods use concentration to maintain awareness. Unlearning the coupling of awareness to concentration may take several months. Maintaining awareness without focusing on an object might seem like a contradiction: by releasing focus, you lose your well-earned, stable calm. Practitioners making this transition may experience a period of disruption that can feel like negative progress before finding a different, more inclusive stability.

Trying to switch from concentration to remaining uninvolved straight away may not work. Instead, think about the transition as a gradual release, as though you are slowly allowing a clenched fist to relax into its natural state.

Some meditation methods comprise a series of instructions to follow mechanically according to your progress on a path. That's not the case with opening awareness. Because of the absence of constraining techniques, daily meditation sessions may be unpredictably varied, especially when you are releasing restraints that you learned elsewhere. This may be frustrating, confusing, and unwelcome if you are used to relatively smooth progress.

Each time you sit, first find where you are. (See the introduction to the *Scaffolding Practices* chapter for an explanation of why this is important.) Try opening awareness first. In particular, spend time finding awareness in arising sensation and external sounds—because those are deliberately neglected in concentrative, renunciative methods.

Rather than deep internal absorption, notice your breath with a light touch, while you remain aware of what else is happening around you and in your body.

See if you can notice and welcome your thoughts as they arise.

Talk to others who have made the transition to opening awareness from other systems. The Evolving Ground community offers resources to help. In our online forum, there are channels dedicated to meditation questions, path journals, and specifically to the opening awareness method, with support from members who have well-established personal practices. After you've spent some time experimenting with the new approach, you might also consider finding a mentor or a teacher who can help answer specific questions.

View

> *One of the most effective ways to transition to opening awareness from other meditation systems is to fully embrace a life-affirming, non-renunciative view.*

Notice when you automatically regard your emotions as problems that must be subdued and controlled, rather than held spaciously with choice. Notice when you regard your *self* as a problem; in particular, the subtle feeling that "something is wrong with me."

The view of the path of opening awareness is that you are basically okay. There is nothing wrong with you.

When you notice negative views of emotions and self, see if you can simply drop them. Find awareness in what is happening, without having to categorize it as good or bad.

Language

In the long run, the language you use to describe your meditation practice affects what happens as your experience develops.

If you make changes to your view and language, it is likely that you'll notice differences in your meditation too. If you periodically reread sections of this book, you will probably repeatedly find that it illuminates aspects of meditation experience you missed on earlier readings.

During the transition from a staged, prescriptive system to an exploratory one (such as opening awareness), it is especially helpful to keep a journal, and to write about your practice.

Notice the language that you use to reflect upon your experience. What words do you return to repeatedly? Do you think in terms of concentration, obstacles, interruptions, distractions?

What would it be like to change your vocabulary to noticing, finding, allowing, including?

Is your language judgmental or friendly? Do you think about your meditation in terms of success and failure?

What would it be like to relax expectations of progress, and instead describe familiar versus new experiences?

Find words that describe the different textures and qualities of your meditation. Is it clear, dull, quiet, noisy, full, absorbed, open, vivid, or calm?

> *I do appreciate how different pithy phrases slice the pie. I've found that as I follow a phrase into practice, the experiential flavors are quite distinct. It's been helpful to swap in phrases based on practice patterns or difficulties I am encountering. For example, the phrase "maintain awareness without manipulation" might be an easier entry point for practice if "remaining uninvolved" doesn't resonate. I could see "manipulation" being a more accessible experience to notice than "involvement." Gathering a whole swath of these phrases could be helpful, especially when starting opening awareness.*

—Tanner, Evolving Ground apprentice

Mixing versus alternating practices

It doesn't work to mix the view, language, and technique of a prescriptive system with opening awareness in the same session. They point in different directions, towards different outcomes. Establish your opening awareness practice on its own terms.

Continue until you are confident with the method and have some results. Once you are familiar with opening awareness, you can see better how other practices impact and change your experience of it.

It is helpful to understand how different meditation methods work and what result they are likely to lead to. Learn about their origins and intended purposes. Listen to the language their proponents use, and discover whether it works well for you or not.

Don't buy the platitude that "all paths lead to the same goal." Empirically, this is not so.

Know the difference between mixing (merging) and alternating (keeping separate) practices. Mixing the techniques from one meditation with another may work, if you maintain consistency in view and want to explore effects. But on the whole, keeping methods distinct works better.

Systems tend to dysfunction when they are randomly mixed up.

Learning Spanish and Italian in the same session without clearly distinguishing them would be confusing. However, some people can learn two languages concurrently when they are clear about which is which.

Alternating different practices is a powerful method. Once you have established opening awareness, practicing other methods in the same session can bring energy and aliveness, keeping your meditation from becoming stale. Evolving Ground meditators practice art, song, visualization, breathing techniques, and physical exercises alongside opening awareness.

TEN

What's next?

Opening awareness is the foundation practice for the Evolving Ground community. All our other practices and programs blossom from it.

Our web site www.evolvingground.org provides an overview of what we offer.

Membership in Evolving Ground is free, and gives you no-charge access to a growing number of resources and meetups: www.evolvingground.org/join

We provide a lively online platform, with many discussions active every day. You will receive instructions about how to access it when you join as a member.

The platform has an area specifically for discussing opening aware-ness meditation. You can bring your practice questions, problems, observations, and curiosity there. Experienced meditators usually respond quickly.

Evolving Ground hosts frequent in-person and online video gather-ings (www.evolvingground.org/gatherings). Many are made available at no charge. For example, the monthly online video *Practice Q&A* session is another good place to get help with any issues you may en-counter in meditation. The informal weekly *Community Hangouts* will give a sense of the community, and some hangouts are also appropriate for discussion of opening awareness. In hangouts, for example virtual sits and topic groups, you can practice and explore along with other Evolving Ground members. They may be thousands of miles away, yet seeing them also sitting silently, or chatting with them, provides a sense of real-time community support for your meditation.

As your meditation practice develops, you may wish to take up one of the paid roles in our community (www.evolvingground.org/roles).

Those include access to more role-specific live video meetups, for example:

- In-depth *practice analysis sessions*

- *Life affirming meetups*, which take meditation insights into everyday life; sessions may include guided meditations, explanations of methods beyond opening awareness, practices for embracing emotions, and exploring relationship as practice

- Our *Evolving Ground Fundamentals course*, a practical, progressive year-long series on the path of contemporary Vajrayana; in each module you explore one topic and take practice experiments into everyday life

- *Member-led programs* and experiential courses exploring vivid perception and confident action

- *Book Club*, meeting twice each month to discuss meditation books chosen by participants

- An evolving set of coach-led *retreats, programs, and gatherings.*

Evolving Ground practices are mainly non-sequential. However, some practices do have functional prerequisites. For example, only when you become familiar with spacious clarity through opening awareness will the instructions for *moving awareness*, a different meditation method, become meaningful for you.

Moving awareness is presence with involvement in perception, sensation, mental events, and all of experience. Through the practice you discover mystery, play, wonder, and awe. I teach courses on moving awareness, and hope to write a book about it as a sequel to this one.

More resources

This section recommends additional discussions—as text, audio, and video—covering some of this book's topics in greater depth.

Opening awareness and spacious clarity

I offer periodic video-based group courses in opening awareness. The content goes beyond what's in this book, and you may find interaction with me and with other students valuable. That's an opportunity for support and guidance, with answers to your specific questions and ways of addressing personal practice challenges. It's also an opportunity to experience the "vibe" of our community, and of the vaster path for which opening awareness forms a foundation. Sign up for my email newsletter at vajrayananow.com/subscribe to be notified of upcoming courses.

Opening awareness is a revitalized, contemporary style of shi-ne, a traditional meditation method. My web page vajrayananow.com/shi-ne-meditation explains more about shi-ne and its place in a broader set of Vajrayana meditation methods.

In our website resources section at evolvingground.org/opening-awareness you will find a growing list of audio, visual, and social resources to support your opening awareness practice.

Spacious clarity is a window into vastness: vividness.live/no-holiness-vastness.

Recognizing different views

To learn more about the origins of renunciative and life-affirming views in Buddhism, read the several-web-page section "Understanding Buddhist Tantra by Contrast" at vividness.live/understanding-buddhist-tantra-by-contrast.

Emotions

Spectrum of Ecstasy, by Ngakpa Chögyam and Khandro Déchen, is a book about meditating with strong emotions. I discuss it at vajrayananow.com/spectrum-of-ecstasy.

Anyone in the Evolving Ground community can attend periodic free "meditating with emotions" groups. We have a reader's guide to *Spectrum of Ecstasy* to help group participants apply the method in their meditation and life: vajrayananow.com/spectrum-study-guide.

I answer some questions about meditating with emotions at vajrayananow.com/meditating-with-emotions.

Basic okayness and unconditional security are discussed (using different terms) in "Your self is not a spiritual obstacle" (vividness.live/your-self-is-not-a-spiritual-obstacle) and "There are no spiritual problems" (vividness.live/there-are-no-spiritual-problems).

Relationship

I teach in-person and online courses on relationship, founded on opening awareness, emphasizing practice and experience. Sessions include conceptual overviews, case studies, explanations of practices and applications, "homework" exercises to try out the methods between sessions, peer group discussions, and opportunities for questions and reflections: vajrayananow.com/kaleidoscope-of-interaction.

"Relating as beneficent space" (vajrayananow.com/relating-as-space) explains in detail how opening awareness practice can transform your relationships, liberating you from fixed patterns of interaction. It's somewhat more abstract and theoretical than the courses.

Healthy relationships are central for Evolving Ground. Members find that community involvement leads to easier, more fruitful interactions and relationships outside the community as well. Our community retreats and in-person gatherings often include introductions to methods for practicing with emotions and relationships.

Transitioning from concentrative meditation techniques

Many of the pages in my *TMI Journal* highlight differences between renunciative concentration techniques and meditation practiced inside a life-affirming framework: vajrayananow.com/journaling-a-staged-path.

I discuss my TMI journal and different frameworks for practice with Michael Taft in "Vajrayana, Engineering, and Jiu-jitsu" (deconstructingyourself.com/rindzin-pamo.html) on his *Deconstructing Yourself* podcast. Transcript: deconstructingyourself.com/vajrayana-engineering-and-jiu-jitsu-with-rindzin-pamo-transcript.html

The web page vajrayananow.com/precision-and-exploration is about language precision and its different function in renunciative and life-affirming meditation systems.

APPRECIATION

Acknowledgements

Ongoing conversations in the Evolving Ground community over the first two years of its inception made this book possible. The shared language of opening awareness is still evolving, as new members bring their experience to our virtual discussions and growing pool of resources. In particular I'd like to thank the Evolving Ground apprentices and other members whose regular contribution to online forum threads have inspired so many to explore a more vivid way of being through their personal meditation practice. The questions and discoveries from those conversations are reflected here.

Ye-tsal Khandro (Kristie Janes) and Donn Vidmar have hosted online opening awareness sessions several times per week for years, welcoming new meditators, learning from them, and bringing that learning to our gatherings.

Ari Nielsen, Max Soweski, Derek Van Ittersum, Andrew Blevins, and Mike Wilkerson brought the kind of energy and enthusiasm to online and in-person discussion that inspires others to practice. Thank you to them for their significant contributions to virtual discussion threads on opening awareness, and to the many others who asked questions and shared their experience, including Rory Mullins, Todd Page, Barine Duman, Tanner Holman, Ignacio Prado, Evan Porter, Vlad Sterizhanov, Adam Strandberg, Jason Murray, Brandon Holmes, James Matthews, Chris Markham, Micha Kosek, Bonnie Magnuson-Skeels, and Christopher Skeels.

Tim Mahan contributed his understanding and information on

practice safety.

Thank you to Phil Weitzman, Govind Manian, and Arthur Joyce for their comments on early drafts of this book.

To Evolving Ground's regular financial supporters: thank you. Your generosity made this resource possible.

Michael Taft's inspiration, support, advice, and encouragement has been immensely valuable.

Thank you to Jared Janes, my friend and cofounder, for the many conversations that inspired translations of Tibetan terms to phrases that reflect Evolving Ground's approach, and in particular for suggesting the term "opening awareness" for our foundational meditation.

David Chapman's *Vividness.live* inspired the tone and content. His encouragement and support, in multiple ways, have made this book what it is.

—*Charlie Awbery*

CHARLIE AWBERY

About the author

Charlie offers classes, community retreats, and one-on-one meditation coaching: vajrayananow.com/about-my-approach.

Charlie's *Vajrayana Now* email newsletter includes practice tips, insights into Vajrayana's relevance to contemporary life, and often short videos. You'll also hear when there are new posts on the *Vajrayana Now* web site (vajrayananow.com), and about upcoming classes and events. You can sign up at vajrayananow.com/subscribe.

Charlie (they/them) was born in the UK and now lives in the US. They first learned to meditate in India as a young adult, when volunteering in development work. Returning to Britain, they studied and practiced traditional Tibetan Vajrayana Buddhism through the 1990s, and took Buddhist Tantric ordination in 2002.

Charlie's primary practice has always been silent sitting meditation, supplemented with Vajrayana methods such as yidam, yogic song, chöd, and combined physical-energetic movement systems. They have also trained in multiple martial arts. Although non-monastic Vajrayana emphasizes spiritual integration into ordinary, everyday life, Charlie has also practiced in lengthy full-time solitary retreats.

After twenty-five years in traditional Vajrayana, Charlie moved on to build Evolving Ground, a community of contemporary Vajrayana practice, with cofounder Jared Janes.

Charlie has worked in international development in Africa, India and the Middle East. They trained in Gestalt psychotherapy and have worked in mental health services and in international human rights organizations. They studied international diplomacy, anthropology, and economics as a post-graduate at the School of Oriental and African Studies and the London School of Economics.

www.ingramcontent.com/pod-product-compliance
Lightning Source LLC
Chambersburg PA
CBHW071138280326
41935CB00010B/1284